THROUGH THE CO

Through the Counselling Maze

ROGER ALTMAN
with CHRISTINE LEONARD

KINGSWAY PUBLICATIONS
EASTBOURNE

First published 1996

Unless otherwise indicated, biblical quotations are from the
New International Version © 1973, 1978, 1982 by the
International Bible Society.

ISBN 0 85476 636 7

Designed and produced by Bookprint Creative Services
P.O. Box 827, BN21 3YJ, England for
KINGSWAY PUBLICATIONS LTD
Lottbridge Drove, Eastbourne, E. Sussex BN23 6NT.
Printed in Great Britain.

Contents

I would like to dedicate this book to my children,
Sara, Ian and Bethan,
for their encouragement, wisdom and humour
while I was researching this book.

Introduction

Personal pain and conflict

One event triggered a complete change in the direction of my life. It happened when I had been in social work for eighteen years, particularly helping disturbed young people at the large children's assessment centre which I ran. I had undertaken a thorough training in counselling, gained experience in that field and, over the twenty-eight years since becoming a Christian, I had also seen the power of prayer as God repaired deep damage in people's lives. I felt secure with good friends and a loving family around me and no major trauma had touched us personally.

However, many things are beyond our control and hard decisions have to be taken which ultimately may affect many people's lives. This particular series of events happened in the course of my professional work, but any kind of counselling or caring is not something we should take on lightly. When tragedies happen the press prowl like hungry hyenas. People in authority may make mistakes or fail to communicate properly, and often no one cares for the carers. When things go wrong, the sense of helplessness can overwhelm and threaten to destroy us.

In 1990 I needed a few days off work to recover after a minor check-up in hospital. Soon after I arrived home, the telephone rang. My deputy at the assessment centre was phoning to tell me that he was having problems with a fifteen-year-old called Philip, who had been beyond control for some considerable time. Now, however, Philip's sudden increase in violence and aggression had brought things to a head.

'I feel we can't contain the situation any longer, Roger. What do you think about getting a certificate of unruliness?' my deputy asked. He sounded upset. I knew he would not have asked for this lightly. We were both only too aware that as the custody centres were full, such a certificate would mean prison for Philip. Yet for the sake of the other children it looked as though the boy would have to leave the centre. We had run out of options.

I thought back to the time I first met Philip. The managers of another Social Services division within the county had referred him to us. From the time he arrived, he was violent towards the staff and harassed the children in the centre. Though he longed desperately for love and care, his continual high-pitched laughter did not help endear him to anyone. In fact his bizarre behaviour concerned me so much that I requested a full psychiatric report on him.

Over the nine months he was with us my concern increased. He stole – one speciality was attacking old women and taking their purses. At the centre he would throw the furniture around and seemed to be wanting staff to restrain him physically. When they did, he became even more violent. We found him carrying lethal-looking weapons ranging from flick knives to hunting knives and I feared that he would harm himself or others. Alarmingly, one day we discovered that he had cut some electric cables.

I wrote many letters expressing my concern to the appropriate people, but nothing happened – partly because Philip needed a specialist unit, and none was available. Meanwhile, all of us at the centre did our best to build a relationship with him. We were having some measure of success and had worked out a programme for him. This involved appointing a key worker for him and arranging flexible education, with periods of time out from school so that he could meet with his key worker and others. He received psychological and psychiatric support and did small group work with other children. He also had help with his interrelationship skills and with working through events in his life.

Then, just as his behaviour was starting to normalise, he absconded. I discovered that his social workers had been promising to place him with a family in the community, who would care for him and give him everything he wanted. To me it was obvious that this would never happen, because no family would ever manage a boy with behaviour like his. Still, Philip lived in hope, and every time that hope was dashed he went wild.

And now my deputy's phone request had posed a real dilemma. After much agonising we decided to go for the certificate of unruliness. When it was issued Philip was sent to prison.

When I became fit enough to return to work I could see that the staff were still worried about how Philip would cope in jail, but at least they could now care for the other children without constant interruptions or danger. Overall, I felt the centre had become a more relaxed place.

Then, after Philip had spent a short period of time in prison, the divisional officer asked if we would have him back at the centre. After a discussion with my management team, I decided that we simply could not take this risk. Anyway, it would have meant special provision since we no longer had a bed available.

They found a place for Philip in a semi-secure unit, but it was not long before he managed to escape. Once caught, he was sent back to prison. Social Services looked desperately for a more appropriate placement, but they were unable to find one. That evening Philip hung himself in his cell.

At the centre it was as if all hell had broken loose. At a time of huge sadness and bewilderment for all the staff and children, we felt the full onslaught of the media, hounding us for a sensational story.

Most of my energy was put into supporting the children in my care – some thirty in all – sitting them down in small groups, trying to help them talk things through. I tried to stay detached and to take on a cool and caring attitude because I also had to help my staff, including my deputy, to work through some of the issues.

We were approached by a team wanting to make a drama–documentary about Philip, but after taking legal advice I decided to have nothing to do with it. Later the programme was shown on ITV – as long and agonising as a feature film, and full of inaccuracies. It brought pain flooding back through the centre, along with a real sense of injustice – towards Philip, towards all of us.

One evening shortly afterwards a fourteen-year-old girl came up to me and asked, 'How are you?'

'OK,' I replied.

'No you're f***ing not!' she said and spent about fifteen minutes talking to me. 'This isn't your fault, or anyone else's,' she continued. 'He lived in a f***ing fantasy world. At least you lot tried to care. But those f***ing social workers – they do the same to me, promising all those things. A family? For him? No way!'

She talked about some of the children we had cared for and reminded me of all the good we had done. I thought for a moment about her. When she first arrived at the centre she had been high on glue, drank a great deal and had been used to sex from the age of nine. Our planned programme had worked well – for her.

'Sure we help some people, but we didn't help him, did we?' I asked. No one could now.

'But you never said he should return to f***ing prison! And as for killing himself, he could have done it b**** anywhere, couldn't he?'

I felt encouraged. This young girl was not always easy to care for, yet she had seen my pain and listened to me.

Eventually the press lost interest in Philip's case, the Inquiry was over and life began to return to normal at the centre. It was not quite that simple, though. This tragedy had hit my whole team head on, causing anguished discussions over professional issues in child care – yet our line management had given us no effective support and we felt isolated from the rest of the county's social work team.

I felt angry that no one had been prepared to listen to us at the centre or to take our advice. I had no wish to pass the buck – we all shared responsibility for failing to meet this child's needs – however, in a sense I felt that the whole system had failed in that it did not take into account the severity of the problem or the lack of alternatives available.

I realised that although I had succeeded in holding myself together for the sake of others, I had rarely felt so devastated or alone. No support or counsel had been given to me, except through personal friends, and because of issues of confidentiality, I could not go into much detail with them. My only comfort was that I had already decided to leave social work, otherwise I am sure I would have resigned there and then. I had spent many happy years working for the Local Authority, but there had to be a better way than this system in which everyone appeared to be a loser and so many were left without the support they needed.

Little did I know that I would be dealing with many similar difficulties and tragedies throughout the UK in the coming years. Even as I write this a phone call has come in asking us to support a family whose young son was shot in an accident, and another from a school where a girl died suddenly. I think also of many I have counselled from the emergency services, who feel so helpless when they are unable to save people in a major accident. I know that the experiences I have gone through will, by the grace of God, help me to support others in their time of need. And I will always remember how desperately I longed for someone to listen to and counsel me in my own personal pain and conflict.

Those who reach out to others in pain – Christians, professionals or whoever – must have skilled support if things go wrong, as tragically they will from time to time in our imperfect world. That is one reason why I feel that we must establish the best standards of training and practice, including proper supervision and accountability. Then we will know that we have done everything in our power to ensure that individuals really do receive the help that they so urgently need.

What is counselling?

Right from my early days as a Christian I have been interested in helping people. It started in the late 60s when my wife and I invited young people from the drugs scene into our home for help and support. Many of these turned up at the youth club or in church on a Sunday evening, but had plenty of spare time during the week. As youth pastor of the church, I was the person they naturally came to when they wanted to talk. Our chats usually took place informally over a cup of tea and a biscuit, a walk or a game of chess.

Many young people drifted into drugs because they didn't know where they were going. Some were genuinely looking for answers to life, or perhaps for a spiritual awakening. They found that the drugs never really satisfied their longings, but as I listened to them and talked about the work I could see God doing in people's lives, I found that many were deeply touched. A number made a commitment to follow the Lord.

That would be an example of 'counselling' at its most informal – 'caring' or 'pastoring' might be better words. It has great and lasting value. Twenty years later, while taking a conference at Bristol's Trinity College, I looked down at the front row and saw five of the people I had helped in those early days. All five had become pastors or mature leaders of well-established churches.

Most of us have caring relationships with friends and family, and share our problems and worries with them at quite a deep level. Those of us in churches may also discuss problems with those who have pastoral responsibility for us, or pray about them with someone after a meeting. Both of these are invaluable in helping many find healing, and both are sometimes loosely termed 'counselling'. However, the word could be misleading, for most professionals would expect the relationships within counselling to be more 'fixed' and formal, due to the use of contracts which establish professionalism and define roles clearly. This particular book is looking at counselling as something relatively structured, where the client has deep or persistent problems. It is primarily concerned with counselling by Christians, whether that takes place within a church structure or reaches out into the wider community.

But what is counselling? Roger Hurding defines it as: 'That activity which aims to help people towards constructive change in any or every aspect of life through a caring relationship, which has agreed boundaries.' According to this definition, counselling can cover a spectrum from befriending and listening through to psychotherapy, but a counsellor is generally thought of as someone in the middle of this spectrum, who is skilled in listening and helping.

Counselling takes place within a trusting relationship where the 'client' feels accepted, non-defensive and is able to talk freely about himself and his emotions. At its simplest, it means befriending in order to understand, to listen and to help someone. The counsellor will aim to provide support and to help the client gain a clearer insight into himself and his situation, until the client can help himself and draw on his own resources – on God's too, if he believes in God.

A trained counsellor should be self-aware, and therefore able to distinguish his own problems from those of his client. Counsellors who attempt to practise without understanding their own strengths and weaknesses are in danger of transferring their own problems onto their clients or else of over-directing them. I believe passionately in the need for high standards of training, supervision, ethics and accountability in counselling – and I want to see Christians out in front in these things, not lagging behind as sometimes happens.

Counsellors need training and often specialist skills, but not necessarily a degree in psychology, or endless academic qualifications, American style. Counselling is a practical 'people' skill, not an academic one. As we shall see, qualities of character and personality and the way counsellors relate to others are far more important than their ability to pass exams.

People sometimes ask me if everyone would benefit from formal counselling. I believe not. Most of us will never need it and there could be situations where it is harmful – for example in severe phases of mental illnesses such as schizophrenia, or where the brain has degenerated, as in Alzheimer's Disease. It could be dangerous for such people to explore their thoughts and emotions through counselling, for they might not be able to cope with the added strain of having past hurts unearthed. Many lay counsellors lack the skills to help those suffering from severe mental problems in a meaningful and constructive way. They must be willing to call on qualified professionals such as psychotherapists and psychiatrists, because hospitalisation or long-term medication and supervision are often needed.

I do believe, however, that there are individuals for whom the specialist help offered by counselling is as vital as crutches are to a man with an injured leg. He will not need the crutches for ever, and in the same way, if counselling succeeds, then people should eventually 'walk' by themselves. Until then counselling can serve both society and the church, since it is all about helping individuals who, if damaged themselves, may have the potential to damage others.

The longest period for which I have counselled someone formally is three years, twice a week, for an hour to an hour-and-a-half per session. 'Ivan', a committed Christian, was already receiving psychiatric help for acute depression. Several Christians well-known for their ministry of deliverance and inner healing had also tried to help him, without success.

Having embarked on counselling him, I must admit that on many occasions I felt like giving up, and so did he. There were times when we said nothing to each other for a whole session; times when he felt very angry, or when he cried. However, I continued to make myself available to him, showing that I believed in him and in the fact that he would come through. During the past six months I have seen a remarkable change in Ivan's life. I believe this has come about because I was consistent and held in there with him, allowing him to find himself at his own pace. He is now doing exceptionally well, and the hospital and psychiatrist have discharged him.

What is this counselling 'maze' and how will this book address the issues?

The whole field of counselling, or helping people through their problems, can seem like a series of mazes. Not only is an individual highly complex in himself, but so are his relationships and the society in which he lives. The counsellor needs to be aware of various channels of help which may or may not be offered – be they legal, medical, or help from Social Services or voluntary agencies. He also needs to be aware of his own reactions and of different ways in which he as a counsellor can help or possibly harm his client.

My aim in this book is to set some signposts by showing how standards of good practice in counselling and training can be established by Christians within both the pastoral (church) and community settings.

First, I tell my own story, which will explain where I am coming from. My years of experience in church and youth work, in industry and Local Authority social work and in counselling and training have helped me gain insight into many things. I hope also that my story will bring encouragement that God is indeed at work reaching out to those who are hurting, especially when we look in detail at one example of a Christian counselling and training centre – Barnabas House – which deals with both pastoral and community work.

Then the book will explore the changes in society and in the church which are having an effect on counselling. Why has the demand for it increased so much in recent years? After considering some of the qualities which make a good counsellor I then take a brief look at some of the different kinds of counselling, particularly focusing on the differences between the pastoral and community settings. I write about how and why the Association of Christian Counsellors was formed and the function of that organisation in setting the highest of standards, thus helping Christian counsellors to find their way through the maze.

In the next five chapters I describe the most common areas of problems which I find clients experience today, and aim to give some perspectives on these. I look at counselling within churches – some of the possible conflicts, and the spiritual helps or pitfalls, especially post-'Toronto blessing'. I outline my vision for the future: to see local church teams trained in counselling and able to draw on specialist centres within their region. We consider the kinds of things which must be taken into account by any group wishing to set up a counselling centre, be this day care or residential, small or large.

Finally, the Appendix acts as a resource file, detailing useful books for further reading or reference, together with some agencies for referrals or advice, training courses and other resources.

Note

I have used true stories of real people throughout this book. However, in order to preserve confidentiality, names and places have sometimes been changed.

I firmly believe in the equal status of both sexes, but I have tried not to ruin sentence construction with clumsy references to 'he or she, his or her'. Instead I have tended to use one or the other. As the majority of the people I counsel are male, I have used the masculine form more than the feminine. I hope the reader will understand that this does not mean I am taking a sexist attitude!

PART ONE
A Journey into Counselling

1

My Own Background

Often a story can illustrate points far better than a weighty treatise – and all the better if it happens to be true! In the midst of a book about a sometimes confusing subject, it is important that readers understand where I am coming from. The experiences I have gained have helped form my opinions on the subject of counselling. I hope that my story will show how I found my way through the maze – both personally and with the organisation I now run.

Early days

I was born in 1944, in Swansea, South Wales, the youngest of four children. My father worked as a military policeman in the Royal Marines. The family was happy, stable and open, and it functioned as normally as any family does, I suppose. I enjoyed life at home. Our family motto was 'If you see it, sell it!' No one minded whether or not it belonged to us! Before the age of five I'd learned to collect discarded coat hangers from the tailors' shops near my grandfather's house in London. I'd bundle them up and help my uncle sell them at Petticoat Lane market. Home was even more exciting, because we never knew from one day to the next if we would have a sofa to sit on or a car to ride in. Life at friends' houses seemed tame and boring by comparison, with no bartering at the meal table or wheeler-dealing over the phone!

In 1948 we all moved to Bridgend in Mid Glamorgan. Soon afterwards I started school and before long learned that a mistake in a sum or spelling brought a clout from the teacher round the back of my small and innocent head. This violence followed a single error as inevitably as night follows day, but my friend Peter and I discovered something interesting. If we got ten sums wrong, the teacher still hit us, but he also danced up and down in an entertaining fashion and turned tomato-red from the top of his balding head right down to his stubbly neck.

Aiming to make as many mistakes as possible did not exactly help my academic progress. As I grew older I saw education as a form of swear-word and, although conforming outwardly, inwardly I rebelled against the system wherever I could. The only thing which interested me about school was sport. Doing well at games not only boosted my credibility with staff and fellow students, it provided a welcome escape from lessons and even an excuse to duck homework.

Not that I became a delinquent adolescent. I did noble things like joining the RSPCA and helping old ladies to cross the road, but still I left school at fifteen with just a couple of minor qualifications in maths and English. My father, in his wisdom, took me to one side and said, 'If you want to eat, you'd better find a job!' I knew he meant it. At that point I woke up.

Fortunately, work was plentiful then and I did not need certificates in education to become an apprentice. I signed up for the next five years with a firm involved in glass and design, while attending art college part time for a year in order to finish my studies. The German-owned glass company which had taken me on was well structured and managed. If I owed them a penny, they wanted it – but then if they owed me a ha'penny, they would pay. I learned a great deal about the work ethic in this highly motivated and skill-based environment.

The firm allowed no trades union, but seemed to have the best interests of its staff at heart. Management believed that every employee, from clerk to building site worker, should experience work in all areas. This meant that someone with at least limited skills was always available to keep production going for a short period, in case of problems. So, while specialising in stained glass, I learned also about mirrors and glazing, crystals and diamonds, as well as general business practice. Later, I became a senior member of staff with apprentices of my own. I am grateful for the way this firm helped equip me for my management role in social work and also for the Christian work which I now do.

Finding God

Back in my youth, athletics dominated my spare moments. By the age of seventeen, I had become a junior ABA Flyweight Boxing Champion and I was also long-distance running for Welsh teams. On Tuesdays my normal training run took me past a chapel at the same time as a group of young people were gathering for a meeting. It was quite a small community and I knew some of them slightly, including Glenys – an attractive girl with chestnut hair from the next village. I'd been wanting to get to know her better for some time.

'You can meet me after chapel,' she'd said earlier that year. 'I don't want my mum finding out, mind!' She was fourteen. We'd met like that on a few occasions and then I'd gone down with a bout of rheumatic fever. While a paralysed arm and leg forced me out of action she and three others from the church group had come to see me nearly every day. We chatted about all sorts of things and had many a laugh together.

A few months had passed since I'd recovered, but now, of all times, when I was out of breath and sweaty from the run, they stopped me and asked a very strange question. 'Roger, what do you think of Jesus Christ?'

Taken aback, I could only stare at them. I knew about Jesus, of course. Though I tried to forget my unhappy days at a Roman Catholic school, I could hardly have escaped absorbing from them endless details about 'Our Lord', or 'Our Blessed Saviour'. My mother called herself an Anglican. We went with her to a very high church on special occasions. I had talked to the priest, but he didn't seem to believe in a very definite kind of God. He married and buried people and took church services, but appeared to look on his job mainly as a way of earning money. By contrast, I found the whole subject of religion rather interesting, perhaps because my father was an orthodox Jew which was different again! When we visited my grandfather, who ran a business up in London, he would tell us long tales from the Scriptures at meal times and on occasions we would attend the synagogue with him. God, not Jesus, featured here of course, but then Jesus was a Jew and so surely I was in a good position to understand his background! Yes, all things considered, I felt I knew more than the average person about religion.

Glenys and her friends weren't asking that, though. They wanted to know what Jesus Christ meant to me.

'Nothing,' I said at last. 'He means nothing at all!'

Undaunted, Glenys smiled and stepped forward. 'We're having a prayer meeting and Bible study in the chapel in a minute,' she said. 'Why don't you come?'

'I don't think so,' I muttered, backing away and then running off as if I had some world record to beat.

The next Tuesday I saw them in the same place, and the Tuesday after, and somehow they set me thinking. When I had been ill and they came to visit me, they never talked about Jesus, but I could see something in them – a kind of peacefulness. Everyone else I knew of around my own age seemed to be searching, arguing, debating and looking for new experiences. Could this small group have found something which the rest of us had missed?

The next week they stopped me again. 'We've a special meeting here Friday,' Glenys said. 'Someone will be speaking and we'll have coffee and biscuits.'

I felt as hungry as ever, and the prospect of food settled it. In any case, by then I had become more than curious to know what was going on. 'OK, see you there,' I said.

Dr Wesley White – a member of the Billy Graham team, no less – spoke that Friday evening. He gave weight to the words he read from the big black Bible. 'All have sinned and come short of the glory of God!'

When he put it like that I could see that a vague acquaintance with various forms of religion wasn't going to do me much good. As Dr White started to talk about the possibility of knowing Jesus Christ in a personal way, I realised what was missing. I needed this person Jesus to come alive for me, and I needed him now!

I found it a tremendous experience, coming to faith for myself. It opened my eyes to a whole new world and brought me into contact with many wonderful people who were giving their whole lives to serve God and the communities where they lived. I found myself attending house groups, young people's celebrations and youth camps, but I still kept up with my old friends and my various sporting activities. I have never wanted to become an inflexible, 'Holy Joe' kind of person. I can't see my sense of humour standing for that! For me the important thing has not been religion, or even any one church, but a meaningful relationship with Father God, who was becoming real to me through his Son Jesus Christ. That deep relationship has continued ever since. Though doubts and fears have surfaced at times and I have lost a sense of closeness to God for short periods, I have always known that his love for me is everlasting.

Youth work

The first thing I did after becoming a Christian was to join Glenys' Elim church. Almost straightaway I started assisting in the Sunday school and then with their young people's work – not that, at the age of eighteen, I was anything other than a young person myself! Looking back, all this activity meant that I did not benefit from being taught within the church. My spiritual growth was stunted by the very enthusiasm of the leaders that I should get involved.

Bridgend was a mixture of large council estates and private residential homes. I noticed crowds of teenagers hanging around the street corners of both types of area. They seemed to have nothing to do. The Elim minister and I decided on a course of action and over the next few months we set up some youth clubs and centres. I threw myself into this, my enthusiasm for sport doubtless attracting some teenagers. Our new facilities were soon packed to capacity. Before long I had become one of the youth directors for Elim in West Wales. Over the next three years I worked closely with other Elim churches in the area to set up ten or so youth centres. We also ran camps for young people during the long summer holidays. I quail now to think of the responsibility I carried as vulnerable young lives were placed into my care, because I lacked both training and spiritual maturity. Thank God nothing went wrong!

I had little time then to reflect on such things. The glass company I worked for was so successful that it could not cope with the volume of orders it received. So at the age of eighteen I started running my own business, employing three others to tackle some of the overflow. We used the profits to buy the church a minibus.

Later, realising that I did need some training, I completed a Youth Community Course at the local technical college. Additionally, I undertook a tough Physical Training Instructor course with the Royal Navy. This qualified me to take the young people on 'Outward Bound' type activities.

It will come as no surprise that Glenys had become my girlfriend. After spending two years in Cardiff doing orthopaedic nursing training, she returned to Bridgend in 1966, aged nineteen. In the October of that year we married. Glenys continued working as a nurse until shortly before our first child, Sara, was born twenty-one months later.

By then I was Youth Leader and Co-Pastor of the Elim church in Bridgend, while my day job designing glassware earned our family's keep. Life was hectic, but then I have always ended up with about three 'full-time' jobs at once! Apart from her involvement in church, Glenys stayed at home looking after the family, as most wives did in those days, but she excelled herself as chief cook at many youth camps.

Our youth work continued to prove highly successful – and not only in drawing large numbers. A real work of God was going on. We saw remarkable changes in some people's lives, for quite a few came to us via the 60s drugs culture. Many who became Christians at that time were highly talented people who are now in full-time Christian work of one kind or another. I remember one lad we called 'Noel the Cornflakes' because he was always the first in line with his bowl at breakfast.

One evening we had requested permission from the police to hold an open-air service at Tenby Harbour. We were refused, so we started a different activity. Then I noticed that some of the young people were missing. It

had been a scorcher of a summer's day, and although the
sun had set for some time, the tarmac still felt sticky when I
found Noel and a group of his friends down by the harbour.
The noise coming from him and the other 'musicians' was
loud and joyful, if decidedly out of tune. I learned later that
they had broken all the rules by holding an unauthorised
singing prayer march down the main street – years before
Graham Kendrick and March for Jesus.

They had attracted a group of several hundred people
who now blocked the entire area – and more holiday-
makers were leaning out of hotel windows. Between
songs, the young people talked about what Jesus had
done for them and Noel preached, becoming so excited
that he almost lost his voice.

Drawing alongside, I heard a woman say, 'This is the
best thing that's happened to Tenby for years!' Just then,
at the edge of the crowd, I heard the crunch and scrape of
metal as one car bumped into another. So far as I could see
no one had been hurt, but I turned to a nearby policeman
and asked: 'Hadn't you better do something?'

'Not now,' he replied. 'I'm listening to these young
people. Good, aren't they?'

I could hardly believe it. That night I knew that Noel
'the Conflakes' Richards would become a well-known
Christian entertainer and worship leader, despite the fact
that he could at that time neither sing nor play the guitar.

What with the camps and all the other activities, Elim
churches were packed with young people and we were
also gaining quite a reputation for helping difficult individuals. Bridgend's Social Services Department took the
unusual step of asking if we as a church would run two
youth evenings a week in their large children's home.

This was my first introduction to young people from
socially deprived backgrounds – children who had been
abandoned in many ways and who suffered from deep
emotional problems. We found that many were desperate

to talk to someone from outside their institutionalised setting. We saw individuals begin to grow and develop. Some joined our church youth club and Sunday school, but this brought its own problems. The first Sunday after we extended an open invitation to the local children's homes the offering basket was passed around the church until it reached the back door, whereupon it made a hasty exit and we never saw it again!

I learned fast. One day I gave one of the lads a few coins and asked him to nip out and buy me some envelopes as I'd just used the last one in the church office. He returned, proudly bearing a box of 500, which had all too obviously fallen off the back of a lorry. He saw honesty as one thing; I saw it as another.

As the young people from the children's home began to trust the church youth leaders, another problem emerged. They would abscond from care and knock at our doors in the middle of the night. Incidents such as these made me realise that I knew nothing at all about the background or culture of deprived children, and I needed to find out fast. My own background and that of the church was middle class. We were firmly entrenched in our own value base. Yet Social Services obviously felt that we had something to offer the children, and they set about training us in some of the skills used in social work and care. In the end funding was made available to set up a number of youth centres in Wales.

By contrast, some people in the churches complained. 'No one has ever been saved through a table tennis ball!' they muttered, darkly.

A new career in Social Services

I was in my late twenties, with two children, when I saw an advertisement in the local paper for a job in Social Services. I felt drawn to it, but at the same time my church was asking me to consider full-time ministry. That would have meant going away to train at theological college. Both jobs involved working with people, and I knew God wanted me to do that. I felt that he was ordering my life to equip me to care for individuals at a deeper and more effective level all the time, but in my heart of hearts I did not feel that God wanted me to become the pastor of a church. So Glenys and I prayed, and I started asking around about the Social Services position.

Outsiders said, 'Yes, go for it, you've got a good chance!'

Someone already working for Social Services warned me, 'No way, Roger. It's a middle-management post. They'll want three to five years' post-qualification experience.'

His colleague added, 'Be reasonable – you've absolutely no qualifications in social work. Even your schooling's not up to scratch!'

On the other hand the advertisement stated that they were looking for someone with experience of working with children; someone who could train them in sporting and Outward Bound activities. I knew I could do that, so I applied – and was short-listed. At the interview I could see that all the other applicants were far better qualified than myself. At the end of a long, long day, I think we were all profoundly shocked when the job was offered to me. It came with conditions though: I would have to go away for training at college and university to gain the required qualifications in social work.

Little did I know what I was taking on when in 1972 I gave up my job in glass design to start my pre-college year as an assistant officer in the largest observation and assessment centre in Britain. At any one time it contained sixty children in residence, with their own school, and between sixty and a hundred staff. I was involved in case conferences, the setting up of individual programmes for the children and also worked with families and school non-attenders. As well as concentrating on the internal management of the centre, I set up educational, staff development and management programmes, working with colleges, universities and other agencies.

On my first morning, a uniformed police constable came to interview one of the children. The headteacher of the school asked whether he had come in a marked police car and, if so, where it was parked.

'Yes, in fact I've brought the Chief Constable's new Daimler,' the policeman said with pride. 'I've left it in the playground.'

'Well, I think you'd better have a look at it,' said the Head, with a sigh.

We all rushed out into the playground and found the splendid new car covered in red paint from front bumper to back. The constable stood there staring and spluttering, too shocked to notice that among the crowd of teenagers milling about, the hands and clothes of one lad were splashed with red.

I discovered later that the Head was not noted for his sense of humour, but that morning he could not stop laughing. 'Your problem, Roger,' he chortled. 'You sort it out!'

My introduction to disturbed adolescents could have been worse, I suppose. The lad had used powder paint, which washed off easily. More seriously, a little later, the same centre school was holding an important meeting with the Head, the Director of Social Services, the Director of Education, the Director of Health and myself. Suddenly we smelled acrid smoke. The children had set fire to the Portakabins and were burning the school down around us!

Then the girls at the local approved school rioted. I was sent, one Saturday evening, in response to a request for more staff. I should have suspected trouble when the Head handed me the keys and walked off. As I entered the building, one of the girls hurled a chair at me. I ducked and it hit a colleague.

In the middle of the night I heard a strange noise coming from above my head. I followed it right up to the attic. Looking up, I saw that some slates had been removed, and at that moment six ropes came snaking down through the hole in the roof to land at my feet. A number of lads from the local RAF station wriggled through the hole and started to shin down the ropes in a professional manner, until they saw me, whereupon they disappeared hastily upwards again. The girls, furious that I had ruined their regular Saturday night opportunity for sex with these men, staged another near-riot.

Aside from the more dramatic moments, I tried, throughout my time in the centre, to see each child as a person, not a problem. I did all I could to get the very best from each one. Of course, I also prayed for them quietly.

In September 1973, after a year of in-service training at the centre, I was seconded to college to gain my qualifications in social work. This school proved much less painful than the ones of my childhood, though one female lecturer surprised me by asking, 'Why do you duck your head right down every time I walk behind where you're sitting? Is there something wrong with me?'

I thought she must be imagining this reaction until my fellow students confirmed that I did indeed bob my head right down low on my desk whenever *anyone* in authority walked behind me. I realised that college must have brought back subconscious memories of my school-days, when any slight mistake would bring painful consequences. Of course, as a mature student I knew perfectly well that this woman was not going to hit me. I'd never seen any of the college lecturers strike anyone – and anyway, I was bigger than she was! After laughing at my inappropriate behaviour, I started to understand how some of the children in the safe environment of the centre continued to react in fear.

After a year of full-time study I gained my Certificate in Social Work and became Deputy Head of the centre, with responsibility for running its education and social work side. I also undertook a one-year Practice Teacher's course so that I could assess students in training. The Welsh Office had built a special training centre for residential social work at our observation and assessment centre. Because of the work I was doing and because they saw my keenness for training, they asked if I would join its Board and become an external examiner.

Following changes in the Children and Young Person's Act of 1969, the models of training were changing. The qualifications for social work had changed in 1970, which meant that there were insufficient people in practice who had them and who could validate training for others. I was invited onto one college's permanent planning group, which led to me becoming an external assessor to four universities and colleges. My responsibilities included assessing their standards of teaching within the areas of health care, social work and education. From 1976 to 1988 Social Services released me from the observation and assessment centre for three months of every year for this work and also seconded me for one three-month period to train in management at the Steel Company of Wales. Both experiences were to prove invaluable later.

In 1975 the Local Authority also seconded me to be part of a team involved in feasibility studies. We were looking at the process and requirements for residential care of children and homeless adults. My first study involved reviewing the work of the Salvation Army and, in particular, some of their hostels. The second was to review the work of the National Children's Home and consider whether their models would be useful for day and residential care schemes run by the Local Authority.

Around the same time my local church asked me to set up larger community centres in socially deprived areas. Because of my Local Authority experience I felt we needed to produce small feasibility studies, looking at why the centres were needed, their optimum size, what provision already existed in the area and what staffing and finances would be required to sustain the projects.

The Local Authority and one or two voluntary agencies saw the value of my small studies and later referred to them when setting up other projects in the same borough or county.

A move and a new job

In 1978 a senior manager's position became vacant, based at a brand new observation and assessment unit in West Wales. I applied for the job, which involved field social work as well as responsibility for the unit's residents. When I was appointed the whole family moved to Carmarthen with me.

By this time I had gained a good deal of experience of working with children. Being in charge of setting up a new unit gave me a chance to do a few things differently. Five out of the twenty staff there were Christians and before the centre opened we prayed in every room. I was also able to train the staff before they had a chance to develop mindsets about the way things had always been done.

One thing I had realised was that children in care all too easily became institutionalised and locked away from normal society. Many had little chance to make normal decisions, such as what clothes to wear, and they had no consistency of relationships and were not treated as individuals. Several highly qualified people would make decisions on behalf of each child – the psychologist, the doctor and a number of social workers. Often these gave conflicting advice, and none of them knew the child very well. 'Lowly' care workers met the children's needs day to day and often knew them better than anyone, but things were ordered in such a way that they never had a chance to voice their opinions to those who made the vital decisions.

I changed things by assigning one key worker to each child – males with boys and females with girls. I encouraged them to develop a relationship of trust with the children and to listen to their stories. As well as helping the children and their families, I enjoyed seeing my staff develop as each realised his or her potential.

As an example, let's take the case of one girl – I shall call her Mary. She had been in care for much of her life and had a history of absconding from both foster and residential homes. She had been expelled from school, she cut or marked herself frequently and she indulged in solvent abuse – probably all cries for help. A number of psychologists had seen Mary, but she did not seem to improve. Because of her disturbed behaviour she had to remain under constant supervision and, even at the age of fourteen, she was never allowed to go into town to buy herself a cup of coffee or choose her own clothes.

I asked Fiona to be Mary's key worker. Fiona was a grade one carer (the lowest grade). 'The most important thing is for you to build a relationship of trust with Mary,' I told her.

Over the next few months, Fiona worked alongside Mary, helping her with everyday things, laughing and crying with her. Soon Mary began to confide in Fiona, revealing a little of her life story.

'I've never told anyone else what he did,' she whispered, in tears one day.

'But these are terrible things which have happened to you, Mary!' Fiona exclaimed. 'Have you mentioned this to your psychologist or your social worker?'

'They're all b**** men,' Mary replied, looking at the

floor. 'How can I f***ing tell them? Anyway, they'd never believe me!'

'Yes. I see how difficult it is for you. But Mary, I think you need some help here. Would you give permission for me to give this information to the team of people responsible for you?'

Eventually, Mary gave Fiona permission. With the agreement of the education department we were able to set up a tailor-made programme which allowed Fiona to spend considerable time helping Mary to make positive relationships with her peers and with adults. A clinical psychologist introduced play therapy, providing large soft toys and cushions for Mary to vent her anger on, and someone she could talk to about her feelings.

It took three years, with great dedication from Fiona, from other skilled workers and Mary herself to work through this programme. Once Mary started to believe that people really were there to help her, she began to talk more about the terrible things which had happened, and then to acknowledge for the first time that they were not her fault. Eventually she dared to believe that she herself had something to offer. Mary completed her schooling and eventually left us to go out into the community, where she did very well.

Time and time again this pattern repeated itself, and it was ground-breaking stuff in those days. The text books we used contained ideas which we now know to be totally incorrect. Some went all out for Freudian concepts, insisting that almost every problem stemmed from the Oedipus complex, where boys loved their mothers and wanted to kill their fathers, or the reverse for girls. The books seemed to take little account of the fact that many disturbed children had been abused.

Strangely, this was also missed by the team of experts who tried to help. Or perhaps it was not so strange. None of them had enough time to build the strong relationship of trust without which such things are seldom revealed. Also, many of the experts were male, and girls who had been abused by men often feared anyone of the opposite sex.

Of course, not every case involved abuse, but many children who found themselves in care had suffered trauma of one kind or another, and no one had really taken the time to listen to them. We not only tried to listen, but to treat the children as individuals and to make sure that each had as much freedom of choice as possible.

I was also concerned about the trauma which children felt if they were suddenly taken away from their homes into care. Often they would experience real grief, not only over their families, but over the loss of a special possession or a pet. Not surprisingly, most felt very angry. I took to giving each one a soft toy. Even the toughest teenage lad would keep his hidden under his bed and talk to it when he thought no one was looking.

The unit was eventually acclaimed as highly successful, and in part this was due to the strong team who worked together for the fifteen years I was there. But I believe that another factor was involved. Soon after we opened, the local fire chief came to inspect the centre to check that we were fulfilling safety regulations. Afterwards he called in to see me personally. 'What's different about this place?' he wanted to know.

'How do you mean?' I asked, surprised by his question.

'Well, the children seem well cared for and happy, but then I visit a number of institutions and that's not unusual. I'd say what strikes me most is the calm atmosphere.'

'My staff are great at caring,' I told him, 'and some of us pray here too. I'd put the difference which you've noticed down to that.'

2

The Early Days of Barnabas

By 1983 counselling began to be introduced to the social work scene. The universities where I was Practice Teacher knew that the subject interested me. Together with a number of Local Authority and government agencies involved with research into counselling, they asked if I would look into what was happening in that field throughout the UK and give an overview of the situation. It was becoming clear that counselling would have a major effect on the country. They wanted to know: does it work?

They also suggested that I should look at some training methods in the USA. Some churches I was working with at the time asked me to use this opportunity to study the work of John and Paula Sandford from the States, whose counselling model involving inner healing had raised controversy in some church circles. I spent time on part of their training and liked what I saw. In fact they soon became friends.

I have to say that overall I found some good quality counselling on offer, both in the Christian world and in the wider community. I concluded that, without a doubt, it does improve the quality of life for many individuals.

The Local Authority sent me on a course in counselling consisting of around 500 hours' teaching and 500 of practice. It was run in segments over about five years and must have been one of the early, pioneering courses in this country. I considered writing up something similar for use in church settings.

Meanwhile, people from outside of my work situation had started coming to see me for counselling. They had heard of me through various means – my job or church work, perhaps. Sometimes, being aware that I had specialist knowledge of certain areas, doctors, ministers or church organisations referred people to me. Others came on their own behalf. It surprised me that most people I saw were professionals – doctors, social workers, pastors, head-teachers, training officers or lecturers. Always busy helping others, people like this had no one to listen to them; no one to help them overcome stress or to begin to find healing for the deep hurts in their own lives, or marriages.

As the referrals became quite considerable and people travelled longer and longer distances to receive counselling, Glenys and I decided to convert some old stables attached to our house into a one-bedroomed flat. This meant that a person could stay and receive help over a number of days.

Time for change?

I was – and still am – extremely thankful for the training I received and for the professional background which has equipped me to help people. I feel very positive about most of my time of employment in local government, but after a number of years its constraints began to make me feel stifled in some ways. This frustration eventually came to a head when young Philip killed himself in prison.

When I first started in Local Authority social work, a friend told me, 'It's the padded cell syndrome, Roger. You think you have room to change things, but you'll soon end up bashing your head against a wall. There's no real flexibility!'

His warning proved over-pessimistic. Being the kind of person who can relate easily to anyone, I learned to be a good manager and I did make changes. However, there were many times when myself or others submitted further good ideas for ways of improving things for those in our care, but sub-committees and finance boards took months or years to consider them, and then nothing happened! Over more mundane issues I was simply told, 'But it's always been done like that!'

Sometimes I ran across those who blocked progress because they resented my success. At other times it was simply that people and their problems did not fit into neat boxes. If the rule book did not cover a particular circumstance, many within the system seemed thrown. Instead of helping, they would invent a new rule, with the result that we moved within a labyrinth of legislation.

I found myself increasingly inundated with piles of paperwork, especially when one of our children was involved in a large Crown Court case. The system worked in such a way that the writing of reports could take priority over the child, or client, or family – who somehow slipped unnoticed into the least important positions. We seemed to be making the maze more, rather than less, tortuous for those caught in it. I was beginning to feel that something had to change; something radical.

When we first moved to Carmarthen I had thrown myself into the challenge of setting up the new observation and assessment unit, and became much less actively involved in church. In many ways my career had taken over my entire life and my faith was at its lowest ebb ever. Glenys still attended chapel every Sunday, partly because she liked to maintain the routine of church-going which she had known from early childhood. Because there was no Elim church in the town we tried various other denominations but, for various reasons, neither of us felt completely at home in any of them.

Not long afterwards it happened that several lively Christian families moved to the town. It was around 1980 and many of the adults worked as professionals in industry, or as doctors or social workers. Oddly enough, none of them settled at the local churches either. Eventually a group of about fifteen of us started meeting in each other's houses and soon formed ourselves into the Carmarthen Christian Fellowship. When around thirty-two students joined us from the various colleges around town, we rented a building. Eventually a group of fifty to sixty individuals met in our house, and they asked me to be their pastor. We were never quite an ordinary church. Almost from the beginning we realised that many of us had professional training in counselling or caring, and that God wanted us to use those skills in a special way.

Then in November 1987 something rather dramatic happened. It started when our phone rang after midnight. This was not unusual, for I was often on call with Social Services. This time, however, the voice at the other end belonged to a girl who had worshipped with us in the fellowship while she studied at college in Carmarthen. She had even lived with our family for a while. After her course finished she had returned to London and was ringing from there now. She sounded distressed.

'Roger, did you see the news tonight – the fire at Kings Cross?'

Glenys and I had gone to bed that evening with heavy hearts after several newsflashes had shown vivid pictures of firemen struggling to rescue passengers from the smoke-filled inferno of the tube station. It was obvious that some people had died, but the number of casualties was not then known.

'Roger, my brother and sister and seven-year-old nephew haven't returned home. We're so worried. Can you pray?'

We did, of course, but between four and five in the morning the phone rang again and the tearful voice of our friend told us that she needed to go to Kings Cross to find out exactly what the situation was. At seven she phoned again, having identified the bodies of all three members of her family.

Never before had I felt such personal pain, helplessness and inadequacy. My professional training had helped me to deal with crisis, but not with anything of this magnitude. We spoke for some considerable time and all I could do was listen and give a few words of comfort. For a number of days afterwards we kept in touch, then she asked if I would come to London to support her and her family.

'And would you be prepared to take the funerals, Roger?'

After a moment's silence I agreed, feeling both humbled and privileged. I knew it would be one of the most difficult things I had ever done. I had never taken a funeral in such circumstances, and never for more than one person at a time – but I realised the importance of spiritual as well as professional input into these suffering people's lives.

Looking around during the funeral service I could see the family with their personal grief and loss, and, behind them, close friends, each with his or her own individual pain. I observed the sadness on the faces of those who represented the emergency services, and it was only too obvious how much the teachers and children from the school the young boy had attended were hurting too. Seeing some of my own personal friends in the congregation, I looked to them for reassurance, for I felt overwhelmed that each person there had different needs.

Some would value the opportunity to talk about their pain, while others would take it inwards and never ask for help. I could never reach them all.

I thanked God for my training. I could say nothing to the family – there was nothing *to* say, and nothing I could do would change the situation. However, I could lend some support, draw alongside them and listen. During the few days I was with them, however, we were continually harassed by the press and freelance journalists eager to get a story. They were like a pack of animals, and their aggressive methods bordered on intimidation.

I had contact with the family several times afterwards, especially with our friend the former student, who for the next two years desperately needed to talk to someone. Although I was used to hearing people's pain day in, day out, somehow the closeness of this experience had a profound effect on me, and on all of us in the Carmarthen Fellowship. God seemed to draw us together and to show us that we had to make more time to come alongside people who were hurting.

I realised how fortunate I had been to have a secure family and good friends. We had suffered very little trauma through the loss of loved ones, except for the death of my father and my wife's father, who had both died in their seventies. But none of us knows what will happen. On the day of the funeral I made a conscious decision that I wanted to reach out to all who were going through times of trauma, and offer them counselling, care and compassion.

However, my time was stretched to the limit and beyond. I began to consider whether this might be the time to think about leaving my well-paid job to give all my time to the work we were doing. If so, where would the money come from? The fellowship had remained small, and could provide no finances to pay me, even if I took a huge cut in wages.

I am not the sort of person who will rush into doing anything. For the next year, ten of us from the fellowship met at six three times a week to pray and ask God what he wanted. We felt that we should not proceed merely because we had a bright idea, an unusual concentration of skills and a measure of past success.

As our private counselling work grew, I worried a great deal about the potential conflict of interest between that and my work in Social Services. What if someone I saw privately later turned up as part of a court case to do with my work? In response to this concern, in November 1988 Carmarthen Christian Fellowship set up a charitable Trust to oversee our residential counselling and other aspects of our care of people. This would call on all the professional and caring skills within the fellowship.

On a practical level I realised that if we were to start some kind of centre for counselling we would need to produce a large feasibility study. This took six months and looked at the need for the project, its suitability within the geographic area and the current counselling provision within both secular and Christian settings. It reviewed the residential care side and the mechanisms of setting up the organisational structure. It looked at financial budgets and the possibilities of obtaining funding from the Local Authority and central government.

Building fund

As the study progressed we concluded that we would need some kind of building for residential and day counselling. Already all of us gave a tithe (a tenth) of our incomes to the church. We decided to tithe on our tithes; to give an extra 10% of them into a building fund. In addition, quite independently, we all made up our minds to put into the fund any expenses which our various employers paid us.

By the end of the year the fund contained about £10,000, which could have served as a deposit on a building, but we were helping a family who had a desperate housing need, and we felt that God was asking us to give them the money. This challenged all our thinking, especially that of the person who looked after our accounts!

Having given some of the money away, I began to wonder if God really did want us to go ahead with our plan after all. Glenys and I took ourselves off to the coast one weekend to pray. I think of my wife as the real prayer warrior, but I found myself down on the beach at six one morning, crying out to God. 'I could ask people for money, but I'm not going ahead on a whim. If this whole thing is right, then I need some kind of sign, Lord. I want some money to come in which I have not manipulated. I don't care how much – 5p would do!'

Returning home, I rushed to open the mail. Unusually, only one letter lay on the door mat. It came from a large missionary organisation and asked if I would go and see them about the possibility of becoming their European director. No, I thought, that's not right, not right at all!

Then the phone rang. It was Lyn, another member of our fellowship. 'You'll not believe this!' she said. 'I've got a cheque here for £500. It came with a note which says, "Roger will know what it's for. Tell him to go for it!" Does that mean anything to you at all?'

I saw at once that this was the key I had been waiting for. 'Who's it from?' I asked her. When she told me the name I knew the woman but had not had any involvement with her for many years. After that, more money started coming in from the group and others. Amazingly, before long we had collected over £10,000 for the second time.

Our family lived in a house we named 'Shalom' – a wonderful place with panoramic views extending twenty-five miles over the Black Mountains and plenty of its own land, including a paddock. We had made the one-bedroomed flat there to accommodate those who needed residential counselling, but a large number of people were waiting to use it. One way forward would be for us as a family to buy a larger property, so that part of it could be used for the work of the Trust, but what would Glenys think about selling our beautiful house?

When I broached the subject, she amazed me by saying, 'That's fine. I already knew God wanted us to sell.'

A hotel came on the market, and enquiries showed that we could set up a legal arrangement whereby, if we bought half, the Trust could buy the other half. This seemed an ideal solution, until surveyors reported that the hotel had dodgy foundations. Then a building which had been an eighteenth-century coaching inn came up for sale. It was situated by a busy crossroads in a small village community within walking distance of Carmarthen itself. I felt happy about this location, as I believe that those in need of emotional healing should not be stuck out in some idyllic retreat, remote from real life.

Though the property market was not very active at the time we put 'Shalom' up for sale, within six weeks lots of people had come to view it. None of them wanted to buy until one day a young man walked up the drive, wearing scruffy jeans and with holes in his shoes. He turned out to be a doctor, and within three weeks he had purchased 'Shalom' for the asking price. Shortly afterwards we moved into the coaching inn, renaming it Barnabas House on the suggestion of someone in one of our prayer meetings. Barnabas is a character from the Acts of the Apostles in the Bible and his name means 'son of encouragement'. We wanted people who came there to find love, encouragement and a safe harbour in time of storm.

Barnabas House

We set about converting part of Barnabas House into a three-bedroomed self-catering cottage, to provide accommodation for those needing residential counselling. The feasibility study became one of the foundation stones for the setting up of the project. We had thought things out carefully and tried to make the cottage as comfortable as possible. One young lady stays there permanently to welcome guests and to clean and care for the house. She also looks after the non-human residents: a veritable garden of indoor plants, two splendid cats, a couple of tanks of peaceful fish and two budgies that chatter in a friendly manner all day long. The lounge area has a television, as do all the bedrooms. Guests have their own cupboards for food in the kitchen, with use of all the facilities, plus tea- and coffee-making equipment in their bedrooms. We give each one a key to the cottage and to his or her own room. They usually come to stay for a week or more.

The fellowship started meeting in the main house and we set aside some other rooms there for counselling. Soon we saw a huge increase in the number of people being referred to us. At first we were amazed. Why should we, right out here in West Wales, have so many coming from all over the country?

We could see one advantage – those with serious problems sometimes found it helpful to be able to talk outside of their own church situations. They could, in a sense, leave sackfuls of rubbish behind in Wales and, on returning home, have no fear of bumping into their counsellors in the supermarket.

Their church pastors and other professionals back home sometimes lacked the specialist skills needed to deal with certain difficult issues, while some of us in Carmarthen had the necessary training and experience. We were seeing every problem which might be met within secular society: acute depression, adult survivors of childhood sexual abuse, eating disorders, stress and burn out, wife battering . . . the list could go on. Many of these people were being referred to us from within churches around the UK. They included full-time clergy and even national leaders. Often they had struggled with serious problems for years and it seemed that we had become known as one of the few effective Christian-based sources of help at that time.

I have come to believe that there is sometimes a place for specialist counselling outside of the local church setting, though, if at all possible, we try to work in co-operation with the client's church leadership.

Training

I became increasingly concerned about the level of bad practice in so-called 'counselling' within churches. This often consisted of a quick prayer, with no follow-up support or time given. If people's problems did not disappear immediately, they carried a huge weight of guilt and a sense of failure. By the time they came to Barnabas House, many clients needed medical help.

As I travelled throughout the UK I found that many Christian organisations were beginning to consider looking at the process of counselling. Although many were happy with the service which Christian training agencies provided, some felt that they had no meaningful value in society at large because they majored on theology and evangelism rather than on any real counselling process. Some Christian models were also being criticised by secular counselling organisations which felt that they were too directive and judgemental. I researched this and although I discovered good in many courses, with a lot of excellent Bible-based training, I had to agree that many did not come anywhere near the required standards for Christians who wished to counsel in the wider community.

In my work as a practice teacher I was developing counselling training for secular colleges. Now I started developing small courses and one-day seminars for training at conferences and Bible colleges. I wanted these courses to come from a Christian perspective and to set good standards in counselling. Although secular training and counselling practice also set good standards and had much to offer, I found that Christians often felt that something was missing from them. On the other hand, I could see that faith and professionalism, running side by side, could prove really powerful in helping people.

Soon various organisations approached me, including CARE (Christian Action Research and Education), Bridge Ministries in Bristol and the Children's Society. They asked if I would be prepared to set up counselling training in local-based churches, covering both pastoral and community work. Before long churches and parachurch organisations all over the country were asking us to give them training too. We were greatly surprised at the sheer volume of requests. Eventually we came to the conclusion that perhaps the very remoteness of our geography prevented us from being perceived as a threat to anyone else's territory.

Whatever the reason I was pleased, because I had a real desire to pass on what I knew. If Christians are to help people find their way through the maze, we must cooperate. I have always been keen to help build bridges and get people working together, pooling their knowledge and resources. I developed courses in various specialisms such as parenting, the setting up of Christian counselling and care centres and the support of adults who had suffered sexual abuse as children. I also designed courses for youth leaders.

A wider vision

The media began to show interest in the work we were doing and we were interviewed by a number of local radio stations about the role of the church in counselling. This helped to bring our work into an even wider arena.

Even so, we anticipated most of the Trust's work as being locally based, but then I was asked to speak at two large Christian conferences. At the first I met a man called Steve Hepden, who spoke a word of prophecy to me. He said he felt that God was calling me to the courts of government and that I would be training across the UK and in other parts of the world. I was to take this thing seriously and be prepared to move into new areas.

I heard Steve's words with considerable surprise, hardly knowing what to make of them. I simply could not see anything like this happening. Putting the whole idea to the back of my mind, I threw myself into the second conference. There a director of counselling from a large church in America approached me and spoke almost exactly the same words as Steve had done. Again, I placed the whole thing on the back burner, which by now had a little flame flickering. Others had heard both prophecies, and were wondering. If two people, who had no connection with each other, had spoken such similar words, did this confirm that God wanted us to do something which would take us way beyond our original vision?

Shortly afterwards, in my role as social worker, I was attending yet another meeting, this time for professionals. A man I had never seen before came up and said, 'You need to consider – take what you've got. It will become much larger. Be prepared.'

This third time I sat up and listened. Returning home I called some people together. 'We need to talk and pray about this,' I said. Still, I felt the weight of responsibility and something in my nature rebelled. I had always seen myself as working behind the scenes. In my experience, organisations which become large and powerful soon cease caring for individuals. In the end I returned the whole thing to the back burner for another three or four years.

It has to be said that a short time after these words of prophecy we found ourselves asked by local government to speak out about a miscarriage of justice, where a person was accused of something he had not done. Then we were twice invited to the House of Lords to talk about our work, especially on the subject of women who had been sexually abused. We were able to confirm that there was little provision nationally for the counselling and care of such people. Suddenly the 'courts of government' did not seem so remote after all.

Extensions

Back at Barnabas House we quickly ran out of space for our work, despite all the new facilities. We dreamed of converting some outbuildings into a one-bedroomed flat for longer-term residential care, especially for adults who still suffered from the effects of sexual abuse in their childhood. For this we needed to raise £9,000.

We prayed and felt that we should take a step of faith and start the building work. The money began to come in, but this time a woman who had suffered a great deal of trauma was in urgent need of housing, and we gave the money to her.

No more cash flowed into the fund, and we were due to pay the builder one Monday in August. On the Sunday Glenys took the family out for the day, while I stayed in the house, praying. Around eight in the evening I found myself out on the patio, drinking a cup of coffee and pondering why we kept finding ourselves in these complicated situations. Had we presumed too much of God? Should I take out a personal loan?

The phone rang. It was a man I had not heard from in a long time. He said that normally at that time of year he and his wife would be on holiday in France, but they had decided to stay behind for a week to pray for our work.

'You know we run a small business, Roger?' he said. 'It's been doing really well. God has blessed us so much this year that we want to give away a tenth of our profits, and somehow we felt that you might have a need. We don't know what, exactly. But could you use £9,000?'

I owed that exact sum to the builder the next morning. The funds were transferred and he was paid on time!

We called the flat 'The Cwtch' – a Welsh word meaning 'cuddle' or 'security'. It offers a bed-sitting room with TV, radio, a fully equipped kitchen, small breakfast area, bathroom and full central heating. Its aim is to provide a safe place to rest, where a person can also receive counselling support on a sessional basis.

Glenys worked as a nurse. For five years in Carmarthen's geriatric unit she had enjoyed talking to the elderly patients and finding out about their fascinating lives. For three years after that she worked as Assistant Matron in a teachers' training college. Maybe because our two oldest children were at a similar age, she got on well with the students. Those with problems would sidle up to the sick bay and ask when Mrs Altman was coming on duty.

Glenys was used to working with all kinds of people. One day, in Tescos, she saw a lady curate wearing a dog collar and it was as though the Lord gave her a little nudge: 'You could do that!'

'Don't be silly, Lord, I'm not even an Anglican!'

'Go and talk to her!'

Normally Glenys would natter to anyone, but now she

demurred. 'Well . . . only if she's still around when we get
to the frozen food section!'

The lady curate remained close by as Glenys piled cans
and boxes into her shopping trolley. When they reached
the frozen food cabinets together, Glenys felt herself go as
stiff as one of the lumps of frozen meat. In the end she did
introduce herself.

'What next?' she asked the Lord.

'I simply want you to consider the possibility of working for me "full time". Don't worry – the dog collar's not
obligatory.'

3

Barnabas Grows

In September 1989, having been trained by working alongside myself, Glenys started as a full-time counsellor at Barnabas House. She was not paid any wages and our counselling has always been free to clients, but she did receive expenses.

Presume nothing – check all things!

That first Monday morning, after our children had disappeared off to school, Glenys gathered with four or five others from the fellowship in Barnabas House. Still unsure about where the bulk of the clients would come from, they began praying earnestly.

'Lord, send us someone!'

'Yes, we don't know who will come through that door, Lord, but equip us, protect us!'

Just then the phone rang, interrupting the flow of prayer. Glenys answered, 'Good morning, Barnabas House. Can I help you?' *It's probably my mother*, she thought.

An unfamiliar man's voice came over the phone. 'Is that Glenys Altman? Oh, thank goodness! My name's Tim. I've just arrived in Carmarthen and I'm in a bit of a desperate situation.'

'Oh, right – well, that's what we're here for!' Glenys sounded most professional. 'You just tell me where you are and I'll send someone round to pick you up.'

While one of the men sped off on this errand of mercy, the rest prayed even more fervently.

'Lord, give us discernment, give us power, give us wisdom this morning!'

The man arrived with a huge knapsack. Glenys took one look at him in the hallway and disliked him. As he enveloped her in a bear-hug she felt even worse, but told herself not to make value judgements. Soon Tim, Glenys and a male colleague were sitting in the front room, sipping coffee.

'Now, whenever you're ready, in your own time, tell us why you're so distressed.' Glenys spoke in her best nurse's voice.

Tim told them how he had lived with his wife in France for the past seven years, working as an English professor.

'Do you know France at all?' he asked Glenys.

'Well no, I can't say that I do!'

'It's a wonderful place. I expect you've heard of the charismatic revival that's going on in the Bordeaux area? No? Well, that's where I live. It's been really exciting. All sorts of people have come over.' He mentioned some well-known names from the Christian circuit.

Glenys nodded excitedly. 'Sounds wonderful! But tell me, Tim, what brings you here to Carmarthen?'

'I'm on my way to Machynlleth, to the Centre for Alternative Technology. I have to bring a group of students over shortly, so I'm doing a bit of a dry run – finding out about youth hostels and everything.'

At that point he started to become a little upset. 'Actually, there is another reason why I'm here. I was hoping that a change of scene might help me get over . . . ' He cleared his throat. 'You see my wife, Freda, she was in her car, in France and . . . '

He had become really agitated.

'It's all right, take your time,' Glenys tried to reassure him.

'It was a juggernaut. Crushed her, the car, everything. All over, just like that!'

He recovered himself a little and managed a half-smile. 'Sorry – it's just that when I arrived here and called into the bank, my wretched trans-cheque hadn't come through. It won't arrive until Thursday, apparently. Seemed like the last straw, somehow!'

The penny dropped. 'Oh, I see!' said Glenys. 'You need some money! No problem. You tell us how much.'

'Oh, I couldn't!'

'Nonsense! By the time you're coming back through Carmarthen your cheque should have arrived and you can return the money then. In fact, why don't you stay here next weekend? My husband leads a fellowship which meets in this house. We'd love you to tell us all about what's happening in Bordeaux.'

At that moment I came in through the front door, a load of files under my arm. Glenys tried to introduce me to Tim, but I whispered that I already knew him.

'Don't be silly, love,' my wife remonstrated. 'He's been out of the country seven years!'

'Can I speak to you in the kitchen a moment, Glen?' I said.

She gave me a look, and mouthed, 'What do you think you're doing?' She had evidently not noticed the nervous way in which Tim was pulling at his jumper.

In the kitchen Glenys rounded on me. 'Roger, whatever has come over you? How can you treat someone like that? He's a broken-hearted man!'

'He's having you on!'

'Roger, do I look green? No one pulls the wool over my eyes!' I had rarely seen her so mad. She continued, 'OK, Clever-Clogs, you say you know him. Tell me about him!'

'All right. He teaches English near Bordeaux, where he says there's a work of God going on – and his wife died recently in a *tragic* accident.'

Glenys looked at me as though I'd experienced some supernatural revelation. 'How can you possibly know all that?'

'He told me – this time last year. You were out working at college. He phoned from the station. Used all the right words, but I'm afraid I saw through him – gave him a tenner and told him to push off. Now I expect he's seen the card you put in the library. He must have got a shock when he realised that I was connected with you!'

Glenys raced back to the lounge, but Tim and his knapsack had vanished. She phoned everyone she could think of to warn them about him, and sure enough, we found out that he had turned up on caring Christians' doorsteps all over the country, with a similar sad story.

We learned a lesson from Tim, which has become our motto at Barnabas House. It is, 'Presume nothing – check all things!' The flip-side of that is, of course, that most of the time we need to trust people, and if ever we lose our sense of compassion it is time to quit. Really, if we are conned out of money, it does not matter too much, but counselling can land us unexpectedly in some tricky corners of the maze, where we need to be wise as serpents and harmless as doves. For example, an individual might spin a tale, and only later would we find out that he was soon to be a defendant in a court case and wished us to testify to his innocence. A lack of wisdom and discernment here could wreck our credibility and thus all the work we are doing.

We also need knowledge of the way social systems and the law work in this country if we are ever going to help people find their way through the maze. Training is therefore vital for those who want to counsel. I will deal with this in more detail later in the book. The point is that setting up a counselling team takes a good deal of careful thought and a rigorous application of standards if it is not to end in a mess of good intentions.

Feasibility studies

In the early 90s a large number of Christian organisations were preparing to set up various projects ranging from residential or day care, to small hospitals and nursing homes, to centres for children's holidays or the homeless or for those with HIV. I received letters from some of these organisations asking if I would complete a feasibility study for them.

At about that time I met Dr Chris Andrews, a Christian psychiatrist from Bethnal Green, who has been highly successful in working with groups throughout the UK, setting up safe homes and centres for those in need. He asked me for some advice about these centres, because they had encountered difficulties from time to time. One reason was that suitable feasibility studies had not been done prior to setting them up.

Since meeting Chris, and later through being involved in the Association of Christian Counsellors, I have completed a large number of feasibility studies and I am convinced that they are essential when planning large projects. In undertaking such studies I have found that many ideas have been too large or simply not viable for various reasons. I have been able to encourage organisations to think again, to relocate or to slim down the size of the project.

Secular groups such as Shelter do excellent research before starting a project. Some Christian organisations, on the other hand, run into problems when they feel that they have heard from God and that therefore their vision as they perceived it must go ahead. Obviously I cannot disagree with them, but I will ask what it is that they have heard. Their heart may want a mansion, but a realistic starting place might be a small cottage or a terraced house in the middle of a city. The principle of 'presume nothing – check all things' needs to work here. I have seen too many groups of Christians ignore advice and invest large sums of money, including their own homes, in a project. When it failed their own lives were left in chaos.

It takes considerable time in discussion with groups to prevent them running into major financial difficulties. I have found feasibility studies successful in giving guidelines on positive and negative issues and on the way the project will work within its environment. I still carry out a number and I love doing them.

Endings and beginnings

In the early 90s I still worked for Social Services and I was not even to be the next to follow Glenys into full-time work at Barnabas House. We had known Lyn Eastwood for years. She played an active part in the fellowship and in the Trust and her husband worked as my deputy in the observation and assessment centre. Now Lyn started working alongside Glenys, learning from her. When Lyn felt that the Lord wanted her to go full time, she could not really afford it. Glenys offered to go halves with her on any money she received as expenses and, in January 1990, Lyn took the plunge.

Not long afterwards, several members of the fellowship, whose jobs had brought them to Carmarthen, found that work caused them to move away again. I had already begun to realise that my ministry was not really that of pastor, although the fellowship saw me in that mould. Nor was I an evangelist – in fact I seemed to be emptying the church rather than filling it!

At that point a number of Christian leaders from both house churches and established churches came to see me and said they felt that God was encouraging me to move in a new direction. Would I consider forming a team to support them in counselling training and in the setting up of projects throughout the UK? They did not want an independent, para-church organisation. All training would be set up by the churches themselves, with us as a group of professionals supporting them. I warmed to this idea and it also seemed to fit in with the three prophecies I'd had earlier.

Carmarthen Christian Fellowship agreed that, as our numbers had been depleted, we needed to concentrate on the caring and training side of our work. We agreed to close down the fellowship as such, and did it cleanly, thank God, without any splits or dissension. Those of us who were left started going to a variety of local churches, but we also formed ourselves into an organisation which we called 'Barnabas House, Wales'. The 'Wales' tag came about, not because of nationalism, but because a holiday centre called 'Barnabas House' already existed.

As the team grew, it soon became clear that we needed offices and the equipment to go in them. In six weeks all the finance came in, despite the fact that we sent no letters and made no appeals. The bank manager asked to see me again.

'I'm interested in your Trust's cash flow, Mr Altman,' he said. 'You do some building and empty your account. Then, when another major project comes along, more finance arrives out of the blue. I can't quite understand how this happens in the midst of a major recession!'

We had several chats. His interest continued to deepen as I explained about the kind of work we were doing. He was intrigued when I told him that we only took on a project when we felt we had heard from God, though we also based everything we did on sound common sense and well-thought-out plans.

'But how do you know when God speaks?' he asked.

'Good question. It's not always easy to interpret and there have been some cliff-hanging moments when I've wondered if we've heard right!' I replied.

Sometimes trying to sort out what is God's will can seem like a maze in itself, on top of all the convoluted practical and emotional problems with which a team of counsellors grapple. So it is good to experience times when he does step in to make everything clear. Often at the last moment, in a way which can appear quite miraculous, he turns a blind alleyway into a nice straight through-route. It is so encouraging to know that he cares and involves himself; that we are not facing an unequal struggle alone. It seems that suddenly all our efforts start bearing fruit.

By January 1992 I knew the moment for me to go full time would come that summer. The timing had been tricky. Eighteen months previously Philip, the fifteen-year-old who had been in my observation and assessment centre, had hung himself in his prison cell. We had worked through many of the issues with the staff and I felt that they would now cope with a change in senior management, but then my deputy applied for a new job and was accepted. I felt I had to wait for his replacement to become established.

By this time I was doing counselling training for the Elim and Assemblies of God Bible Colleges, for CARE, Youth With A Mission (YWAM) and many other church groups around the country. I was helping churches set up day care and small residential counselling centres, as well as counselling individuals myself. The work load had simply become too great for me to cope with running the observation and assessment centre as well.

A number of people offered to support me financially, which would have provided income totalling around a third of my normal salary. On paper I knew this would not work. I had two children at university who were ineligible for grants, as these were assessed on my previous year's earnings. Also I had three of us to feed and clothe at home, plus a mortgage – to say nothing of running the two vehicles which were essential for all the travelling we did.

However, I decided to hand in my notice in May. Though I had said nothing, shortly afterwards Social Services announced that they were about to give me a higher grade, which meant a large rise in salary. This came as a shock to me, for I felt I was earning enough already.

At Spring Harvest – the big Christian holiday conference – I heard Sue Mitchell from Ichthus speak about the call of God on people's lives. 'Often we worry about what we have to give up – our pensions, our security . . . '

That's true, I thought, knowing that my pension would be frozen and that I would not receive any redundancy package. 'Couldn't you get them to give me the sack, Lord?' I muttered, but sensed that the answer was 'no'. I had to take the decision, in full awareness of all the implications, and trust God.

When I told people at work they were shocked, both the directors and my colleagues.

The Inland Revenue rang my accountant. 'He's moonlighting, isn't he? No one gives up a job with that kind of salary to go and work for God!'

The simple fact was that most of the churches we were helping could not afford to pay us, so Glenys and I had started 'living by faith' as far as finances were concerned, and the first thing I realised was that I knew nothing about faith! Always comfortably off, I had been used to giving to others. Now I had to do something much harder: I had to receive from others' generosity all that I needed to meet the basic needs of myself and my family.

I have to say that God was good. Finances did come in. Our son and daughter at university finished their courses and we maintained a reasonable standard of living. All I know about stress tells me that worries should have crowded in to keep me awake, especially as I was working twice as hard as ever, but God has helped me to relax into trusting him. Remarkably, every night since I left social work I have slept like a log.

Straight after going full time I found myself travelling all over the UK, and abroad too. I drive around 80,000 miles in twelve months – such a high mileage that I wear out a car in two years! There is so much demand for training in Christian and some secular settings.

Also we started being invited to a number of countries in Europe, the USA and Africa. For example, in Germany I addressed 600 doctors and psychotherapists from many nations on the subject of adults who were sexually abused as children. We have helped with trauma work in Bosnia and AIDS work in Uganda.

Television, radio and newspapers in this country continually asked for my opinion or wanted me to appear on programmes, and some of them came to film or record our work at Barnabas House. Many organisations were putting me under pressure to write books and training manuals or to produce audio or video tapes. Colleges, police forces and other branches of the emergency services were inviting us to run day conferences and seminars. Probation services, doctors, psychiatrists and lawyers were asking for our support. I thought back to the various prophecies I had received – and wondered.

Christian Resource Centre

Back home the next big challenge came when we were running short of space again. In early 1994 a disused chapel a few hundred yards from Barnabas House came on the market. It was just the right size to provide the four small offices we needed, with some counselling rooms and day-care facilities, plus a seminar room in which we could train up to forty people.

I went to see the bank manager and explained the situation. 'We have no money, but we're praying, and we believe that God wants us to have this building. We've thought out all the plans and we'll budget carefully.'

'Fine,' he said. 'I'll play safe by taking a look at the building, but I believe in what you're doing. Don't worry about it. I'll cover you. The only thing is – can you give me some warning of the moment?'

'What moment?' I asked, puzzled.

'You know, the moment at the eleventh hour when you'll give all the money away!'

There was no answer to that.

And so the building and conversion work began on the derelict chapel. Money started flowing in from all over the country, including £20,000 in a single donation from Northern Ireland. We called the place 'Barnabas Christian Resource Centre'.

Today, I am Co-Director of Barnabas, though I am often away. Part of my role there is to give advice on the Children Act, Child Protection procedures and the setting up of Christian counselling centres within both pastoral and community settings.

At Barnabas House and Christian Resource Centre we now have a team of around twenty people. Our residential accommodation is booked up far in advance, probably because few facilities like it exist in this country. Barnabas House Trust deals with both residential and day care and counselling, and with family work and counselling. Glenys heads up this part of our work, co-ordinating who should counsel whom, or making referrals, so that someone likely to require long-term help can be counselled closer to their home. We often ask that someone coming from a distance should first send a letter telling us a little about themselves and their situation, so that we can best assess who should counsel them.

Lyn does some counselling, but mainly acts as my PA. Two people work in the office, on secretarial and reception duties. We have another two team members involved in training, plus research and development – writing courses, compiling a counselling directory, etc. Another full-time team member deals with the accounts and other financial matters. As the work grew, we found that rules on the financial implications of charity status, or where to apply VAT could prove an enormously complicated part of the maze, and it is vital that everything is handled properly. Because of my own family background, where things were bought and sold not strictly by the book, I was aware that I needed to be extra careful in avoiding any temptation in this area.

A whole team of trained people do voluntary counselling on a sessional basis. Because many people who live in the Carmarthen area speak Welsh, we have at least a couple of counsellors who are fluent in that language, and trainers too, for those Welsh-speaking churches which invite us. It is important that wherever we find ourselves, we are sensitive to the culture around us.

From the beginning we worked hard at setting the best standards we possibly could. Not that we wanted to be the all-singing, all-dancing answer to everything, but from my experience in social work, I realised that we needed a strong structure built into this organisation. We needed to spell out our aims and objectives and give clear guidelines to our staff – about those we could counsel and those we should refer on, for example. I saw a need for regular staff meetings, integrated supervision and both in-house and external training. The staff needed to know that they were accountable to the directors of the organisation – Glenys and myself. We were in turn accountable to the board and trustees, which included external members. It was also essential to have a code of ethics and a complaints procedure.

The aim of the Trust is to help and support those in need and to train others to do the same. So much has been given to us that we have always felt it important that the Trust gives all of its services free or at cost. Therefore we give away our income from the sale of books and so on to various projects in the UK and abroad and also support one worker in our organisation.

We felt it vital, especially when helping people from the wider community, to make it clear that we are a Christian organisation, so we called ourselves Barnabas House Christian Counselling Centre, to avoid any chance of confusion or hidden agendas. About 40% of our work involves people from the wider community. Some have asked specifically for Christian counsellors, or maybe Christians who have tried to help them have recommended us. I find it amazing how many come to know God for themselves later, even though we have not mentioned him at all. Of course, we pray for them, though not out loud.

Prayer will always be a major part of our work. We set up a team of intercessors from all across the UK. The regular prayer letters we send them give no personal details of clients, but we find that God directs his intercessors how to pray, and we could not do what we are doing without them.

From time to time team members themselves may need counselling or support. I realised that, especially for major problems, we would need to call on people from outside of our organisation to do this. I also invited local Christian leaders and speakers to encourage the team and minister to our spiritual needs. Team members now attend different churches, but we meet on a regular basis for prayer and worship together, and the seminar room at the old Salem Chapel has proved a great asset in this respect. A real family atmosphere has developed among the team, and it is vital that we care for each other.

Barnabas Training Consortium

The old Salem Chapel is also the home base of Barnabas Training Consortium, headed up by myself. It is responsible for training, research and development, feasibility studies and working with colleges and church agencies. We now train over 3,500 students a year on our various counselling courses around the country. We do some of the counselling training for Youth With A Mission, Elim, Assemblies of God, Pioneer, the Presbyterian Church of Ireland, CARE and CFC Belfast. We also provide training courses for individual churches of many streams – Anglican, Methodist, Baptist, charismatic. I am a trainer for CWR and Consultant Trainer for CARE and Premier Radio.

We are in the process of implementing field trials prior to setting up six training centres linked to Barnabas Training Consortium. High quality Christian trainers will be based in London, Scotland, Belfast, Brentwood, the Pioneer network of churches and Carmarthen. We are training these trainers, whom we expect to have at least three years' experience in counselling. We prefer those with a background in social work, health care, or those with pastoral or teaching diplomas. We will license out our BTC training material to the centres and monitor their training. Eventually they should be able to teach all our courses from basic to advanced level counselling, team building and training the trainers. They will also be equipped to take specialist courses such as child abuse, or ones for the general public such as parenting.

People sometimes ask how trainee counsellors gain the hours of counselling experience they require for accreditation. The more advanced counselling courses provide opportunity to counsel fellow students over real 'live' situations as well as in role play. Then within their church or counselling centre students sit in with an experienced counsellor who gradually allows them to lead sessions under supervision. The same thing happens in social work where a trainee will at first work alongside a qualified social worker, gradually taking over some of his case load. Doctors and surgeons, or anyone from a practical profession involving people, have to train in this way and their patients or clients are normally happy. In the case of counselling, the courses will help with trainees' understanding, especially the important point of understanding themselves, so that they do not project their own problems onto clients later.

PART TWO
The Changing World of Counselling

4

The Shifting Maze as It Affects Society

Why has counselling become such a growth area? Why has the demand for it grown so dramatically over the past decade or so? I believe the main reason is the huge changes within both society and individuals, which have made life ever more complex and pressurised.

Changes in society

Isolation

As I was growing up, if I had a row with my mum I used to run down the road to tell an aunt the sorry tale. She would give me a slice of home-made cake and a cuddle, then lend a sympathetic ear, and soon my world would feel fine again. Right through into the 50s most families had armies of aunties, or other members of their extended families, living locally. Many wives stayed at home, where their common sense and good listening skills provided wonderful safety valves for their family and for neighbours too. People went through all kinds of terrible things in the war, but most never needed counselling because their families or communities pulled together and helped and supported one another.

In times of tragedy I find that people can still pull together, and neighbours who have never talked to each other will offer great support. However, I have met many people in recent years who say that they have no one they can really talk to. That surprises me, but perhaps it shouldn't. After all, we charge about in cars now instead of walking down the street and stopping to chat to one another. We queue in silence at out-of-town supermarkets, our blank stares meeting only those of strangers. We tend to watch TV and videos or play computer games in our homes instead of joining in more sociable forms of leisure activity. The sound of a human voice asking, 'How are you?' over the telephone used to add a little warmth to the office day. Now, instead of phoning a contact or making a personal visit, we fax companies or send electronic mail from one computer to another.

Most of us have moved right away from the place where we were brought up and may have no members of our wider family living anywhere near. We embark upon the daunting task of parenthood, perhaps having held a baby only a couple of times in our lives and with no experience of looking after our young terrors of cousins or nephews. Grandparents and aunts no longer live just round the corner to give us a break or a cup of coffee and a sense of proportion.

Many people travel some distance to work and grumble that there is no sense of community in the place where they live. No wonder large numbers feel isolated, above all those on estates where they fear to venture outside after dark. Churches once formed a natural meeting place and help could be found there, but most are locked these days, while the newer churches, being centred more on people than on buildings, can prove hard to locate. Many are locked out by the church in a more subtle way when, rightly or wrongly, they perceive that 'religious people' condemn them as not good enough.

Men in our society tend to think they have to be macho and will talk about cars or jobs or women, but won't share their own problems, struggles or weaknesses with anyone. Perhaps this is why men come in ever increasing numbers for counselling.

Whatever its cause, isolation deprives people of safety valves. Often emotional problems can be overcome in the early stages with the application of a little tender loving care. Where people live in effective isolation, though, problems can build up inside until they explode like a very messy and destructive volcano. Afterwards a good deal of counselling or even medical skill may be needed.

Coping with change

Over the past twenty years the pace of change has accelerated faster than at any other time in history, leading many to feel insecure or stressed. I first noticed in 1976 that great changes were coming, and I saw that they would affect many areas, from academic institutions to health care. More recently our society has been plunged into a state of uncertainty by the upheavals of privatisation, along with the collapse of our traditional industrial base and the huge technological changes which affect us all.

Both the law and the great social institutions are changing. Suddenly we as individuals find ourselves responsible for the complicated business of choosing a pension scheme, or deciding whether or not our children's schools should go grant maintained. We have to cope with uncertainties about the National Health Service and other parts of the Welfare State. Many now pay private charges because no local NHS dentist has space for them. They worry about how they will manage when Granny needs looking after, or how to help their teenagers who are scraping an existence at university on student loans. For most of us the maze of life has become a great deal more tortuous and confusing as many of our former certainties disappear. If a parent is bringing up children alone, issues such as these can appear almost overwhelming.

Many people also struggle with huge changes at work. They often feel they have to put in longer and longer hours, which leaves little time for family and friends or for recreation and relaxation. An engineer friend of mine was standing by a trench in the road one day. Something had gone wrong and he was discussing the complicated technical problems with his colleague when a workman emerged all muddy from the hole and joined in. He knew what he was talking about and soon the three of them had decided exactly which materials were needed.

'But how do you have all this knowledge?' my friend asked the workman.

'I trained as a quantity surveyor, and I was a good one, always rushing off on some project or other. Then one day I realised I had no time to do anything else, so I chucked it in. Now I work hard for eight hours a day, see my favourite people in the evenings and sleep well at night!'

My friend commented on how unusual it was to find someone prepared to take that course of action.

Forty years ago people may have worked harder physically, but their lives were less stressful and hectic. This was partly because they had a lower, more realistic level of expectation. Family or human issues were seen as more important than material possessions. Today most of us get caught in the rat race. As the work pace quickens, breaks for tea and biscuits are becoming a thing of the past. With them goes the opportunity for a good moan or laugh, or maybe to sense that a colleague is feeling down and needs a little support. More safety valves bite the dust!

The other day I saw some computers being installed in a university. Commands are spoken to them, then dictation is quickly converted into a beautifully laid out document which spews out of the printer with all the correct spellings and grammar. I am told that hospitals, solicitors and other professionals are showing great interest in this system. I wonder if in the future people may say, 'Bye

bye, secretaries; hello, super information highway!' and cruise it for weeks without ever meeting another human being.

While secretaries and others may find that their training and skills have become superfluous, many feel inadequate in a different way because they are expected to acquire vast new areas of expertise on the job. The face of many working environments has changed, and not only because of computers. A doctor suddenly has to cope with his practice becoming fund-holding. Overnight and with minimal training a headmaster finds himself with responsibility for the finances of what is effectively a multi-million pound business. A solicitor, whose small practice depends on conveyancing for its bread and butter, plunges into debt because houses are not being sold, and needs to search out other areas of law in which he can make money. No wonder that an increasing number of professionals are seeking help from counselling. For who else listens to the headteacher or social work director under stress? Many are reluctant to discuss their feelings of inadequacy with colleagues for fear of redundancy.

Redundancy

During the late 70s and early 80s, society became very materialistic and many individuals went all out for what they could get. Young people received high wages which they put towards a deposit on the latest car one month and a double-glazed conservatory the next. In the absence of any religious belief they swallowed the advertiser's message that if they wore the right labels outside of their clothes and were seen in the right places, then all would be well for them in a Thatcherite Utopia. When the economy plunged suddenly into depression, their world fell apart. Weighed down by huge debts, many realised that their possessions were not as valuable as they had thought. Redundancy, or the fear of it, threatened their bed-rock of belief in materialism. They could only watch as the gulf between rich and poor widened, and panic lest they found themselves permanently on the wrong side.

A swathe of industrial closures, from mines to steel-works, has brought a sense of hopelessness to whole communities in Scotland, Wales, the Midlands. . . . At least manual workers often have certain street skills and a willingness to do menial tasks. They tend to adapt more readily than professionals and middle management do when they suddenly discover to their great surprise that there is no such thing as a job for life. Skilled people of middle age or above may be unlikely to find similar work again. To them the thought of retraining in a different field can seem like an impossible barrier. They tend to lose all confidence, becoming depressed and apathetic or developing psychosomatic illnesses. It is often not until that stage that someone thinks of asking for help from counselling or other sources.

The kind of help people look for

If a person's general level of insecurity increases due to some of the pressures mentioned above, eventually his more personal problems may come to the surface and demand attention. Those who fail to find effective help elsewhere might become desperate enough to go to their GP. On average, 20% of a GP's patients will be suffering from some form of depression. Others turn to counselling, perceiving it as a less threatening solution than medicine or psychotherapy.

Apart from the very rich and Americanised who were proud of having 'therapy', most professionals used to feel that they would bring stigma upon themselves by asking for help. In the past, statutory bodies and church-based initiatives worked mainly with those from socially deprived backgrounds – for example with the homeless. Now it is clear that other social groups need help too, including those in our predominantly middle-class churches.

Changes for the individual

We are more aware of issues

Counsellors are certainly dealing with an ever increasing workload. In fact it could be said that counselling has become a growth industry. Does that mean that all of society's problems are getting worse? Not necessarily. I believe that counselling is coming more to the forefront because individuals within our society are more aware of issues. This has its positive and its negative side.

On the one hand I believe that we suffer from an overload of information about every form of aberrant behaviour or psychological disturbance. The problems which are mentioned on day-time television astound me. Thirteen-year-olds today know more than I did at twenty-five!

All of our stress levels rise as we worry about obscure and frightening things which are unlikely to happen to us, or to anyone we know. We can become a bit like the man in Jerome K. Jerome's *Three Men in a Boat*. After reading a medical dictionary, he concluded that, with the remarkable exception of housemaid's knee, he had every disease known to man – in fact he should have died already from a large number of them! In a similar way, after exposure to some sensational programme or magazine article, someone who used to enjoy dressing up during his childhood might start to wonder if he had transvestite or even transsexual tendencies. A mother might panic that a daughter who has been a bit off her food for a few days is becoming anorexic. Many parents will not allow their children the freedom and healthy exercise of walking to school because they fear that a molester hides behind every bush.

It is not true that all society's problems are getting worse. Take sexual abuse of children and domestic violence, for example. It is clear that these things have always gone on. Most experts think that per head of population, no more children are being abused, no more wives are being battered now than there were ten, twenty, forty or sixty years ago. So it is not so much that society is changing, but simply that more cases are reported, which must be a good thing. More people are seeking help because they recognise that such subjects are no longer taboo. For the first time in their lives, they reckon they stand a chance of being believed and treated sympathetically. In particular the movement towards the liberation of women in our society means that many are no longer prepared to put up with the terrible things which their mothers or grandmothers endured in silence.

Publicity for the work of organisations such as Child-Line has given many individuals who really are hurting the courage to come forward for counselling. Counselling has become much more acceptable and widely known through the good work of organisations such as Relate (formerly the Marriage Guidance Council), Cruse (bereavement counselling), the Samaritans, Alcoholics Anonymous, etc. The media have played a positive role in making individuals aware of the possibility of help. There are adults who may never have told anyone the trauma they suffered years ago, but who have tried to bury the memories as though nothing happened. One woman came all the way from Sweden to our organisation in Wales for counselling.

'I don't know why I've come,' she said to Glenys. 'You'll not believe me, no one ever has.' As she told Glenys how she had been sexually abused as a child she began to find acceptance, help and healing.

Increasingly clients come ready to reveal the real root of their problems rather than simply saying, 'I'm depressed,' or, 'I'm bad tempered with my family these days.' At the time when the news and various documentaries focused on child abuse cases in Cleveland, I was surprised at how many Christian women came forward.

They would say something like, 'I was watching this programme and suddenly I felt so upset I had to find help. I've always known that I was abused as a child, but that was in the past and I've tried not to let it affect me. I mean I've got to hold my marriage together, haven't I? But I've reacted so strongly to all this talk about Cleveland on the TV, I've realised I can't push it all down any longer. There is help, isn't there? I need it!'

Changes in counselling training

Because counselling is such a growth area there is a worrying trend for people to set themselves up as private counsellors with minimal training and no accountability. At present nothing stops them discrediting counselling in this way, although it looks like change is on the way.

A number of groups and academic boards are at present reviewing the whole subject of counselling qualifications. There has already been much research and development – for example with the new National Vocational Qualifications which are intended for those working in statutory and secular bodies. At present there is no standardisation in training, which means that both professionals and lay people can be confused about the levels required. However, good courses should be recognised by the British Association of Counsellors or the Association of Christian Counsellors, and can be found in colleges, universities and other places. I find it encouraging that the development of counselling standards and training is being taken seriously at all levels.

The demand for counselling, and therefore for training, has never been greater. I believe this has to do with the way the walls of the maze are shifting, due to the changes in society which I have described above and also to changes in the law. Examples would be the new Care in the Community legislation, the Children Act and new guidelines on accreditation of counsellors. These are discussed in more detail elsewhere in this book. For the current position of counselling and accrediting organisations in British and European law, see the end of Chapter 7.

Since the launch of the Community Care Act, the government has encouraged Local Authorities and other statutory bodies to contract out for the services they need. Some large companies or organisations have started employing counsellors – for example the emergency services now make them available for post-trauma work with staff.

Also many professionals – including doctors, social workers and educators involved in pastoral care – are realising that they are not themselves trained counsellors. They wish to make referrals to those who are. More GPs, whether fund-holding or not, are wanting counsellors as part of their practice; so are Health Trusts. Many colleges are asking counselling agencies to contract to them – some schools too, though in many parts of the country schools are still relying on the psychological services provided by their LEAs.

Because of changes in society, individuals are also coming forward for counselling training. Some realise that neighbours or family have problems which are way beyond their present power to help. A number have been through a traumatic experience themselves – a divorce or bereavement, maybe – and wish to come alongside others who are suffering in a similar way.

With all the changes in the shifting maze, ongoing training and supervision become particularly vital. Counsellors must be accountable to their own professional organisation as well as to those who contract for their services. They have to prepare for the likely new regulations as well as upholding certain standards which should ensure that they bring a measure of healing rather than further damage to their clients.

It is not difficult in the light of all this to see why the demand for counselling training has mushroomed over the past five years. Such is the concern to see well-trained counsellors in place, that finance has become available. Some comes in the form of student grants, the rest through the support of courses which have sprung up in colleges of higher education, universities, community care groups and also in church-based organisations. Recent research has shown that all major courses are fully subscribed and often have considerable waiting lists. Those run by my own organisation are fully booked for several years ahead.

5

The Shifting Maze as It Affects Christians

When churches, and especially cell groups, are caring, honest and work properly, many people find healing for their emotional damage without ever needing counselling. Most churches have a great asset which I call the 'sticky bun brigade' – ordinary people, who, if mobilised by the Holy Spirit's and/or leadership's prompting, can come alongside others who are hurting. They offer friendship and a listening ear, along with maybe a walk in the country, a cup of coffee or some practical help.

However, in my work over the past few years both at Barnabas House and as a freelance counsellor, I have been surprised by the massive increase in the numbers of Christians and full-time church leaders who seek our counselling help or support. Many are referred by doctors or solicitors, by professional bodies or by churches, while some refer themselves. I have thought a good deal about the reasons why so many come.

Recent changes have encouraged more Christians to come for counselling

Maybe for the first time in living memory, such realities as redundancy and the increasing divorce rate are hitting

church-goers. They might experience major marriage problems, emotional disorders or work- or stress-related
issues; they might be involved with conflicts in church
situations or even with fraud. We have also seen large
numbers of Christians, both men and women, who have
been sexually abused as children. In other words, the
problems are often identical to those found in the wider
community. In the past, however, they remained hidden,
because Christians did not talk about those things. To do
so was to admit failure.

At one time, if anyone in my church asked how
another member was, he or she replied, 'Fine!' After
all, we sang in church about how Jesus died for us and
how much the Father and Holy Spirit did for us day by
day. It would have sounded ungrateful not to be fine,
wouldn't it – especially after hearing that rousing ser-
mon? Still, the fact remained that underneath their smil-
ing masks, many were not fine but were experiencing
inner turmoil. They might have felt sad for some very
good reason, or pressured or worried, but, convinced that
Christians should never have problems, they tried to put
on a brave face and leave their bad feelings at the cross.
If this failed to work, guilt added its burden to the
weight they already carried.

Of course, what Jesus accomplished on the cross does
have great power. Some people do shed sins or problems
overnight when they become Christians. My temper used to
flare up easily before I started to follow Jesus. Afterwards,
though I have occasionally felt that I could have let fly, it
ceased to be a major area in which I struggled. However,
other things take longer to work through. These include bad
attitudes and sinful habit patterns, damage from the past
which causes us to relate to others in less than helpful ways,
and anxieties about the present or future.

Sometimes when we pray God puts things right at once;
at other times our pain is too deep. It has to be first

identified, then worked through at a pace which each individual can manage. Those who fail to do this, and continue to mask or push down their negative feelings, can develop a psychosomatic illness or slide into depression. These things may often be prevented if people are prepared to talk about their pain; that is provided someone else is available to listen – not necessarily to counsel, just to listen.

A new honesty and a safe place

Thankfully, some of the positive changes in society at large are filtering through to Christians, many of whom are now prepared to be more honest and talk in more depth to one another than has been true in the past. Good teaching has percolated through to many churches, which again explains why more Christians are coming forward for pastoral care and some, eventually, for counselling. To admit to having a problem is no longer seen as a denial of faith.

Many hurting Christians are no longer content to sit back with a 'Bible verse plaster' to cover their festering wounds, or even their sins. If a mature, spiritual Christian has just committed adultery he already knows that 'all have sinned and fallen short of the glory of God'. He has probably learned the commandments by heart and certainly does not need to be told, as one or two people I know have been, that 'all adulterers go to hell'. Nor will he necessarily wish to talk about his conscience with a secular counsellor who may not understand.

Many people are looking for a safe Christian setting within which their personal conflicts and emotions can be dealt with in an appropriate manner; where they can have time and space to think and talk through all the implications. It will not help to be too directive in telling the person what to do. Forcing change is even worse. The danger is that the person will see such 'help' as something done to him, not something which he has seen, owned and experienced for himself.

A Christian counsellor should know that people need to repent, where appropriate, of sin, but that it needs to be their own repentance, not something imposed on them from the outside. Afterwards, when the wound has been thoroughly cleaned and attended to, prayer or Scripture may further the healing and provide a barrier against further hurt or reinfection. A Christian can take the process further than a secular counsellor would.

The true story of 'David' will illustrate some of these points. A senior educationalist in a very large department, David found himself going through deep bouts of depression over a period of nearly two years. In regular contact with his doctor, he was also seeing secular counsellors, but, as a Christian, he felt a little concerned about some of the methods they used. Though these were termed 'non-directive' he sensed a great deal of prejudice towards his Christian faith. When it was suggested that all his problems stemmed from his belief in God, he questioned the code of ethics of the organisation under which his counsellor worked. After several weeks he told his GP that progress was hampered because he felt unable to express his own value base to his counsellor. The doctor suggested that he sought help from Christian counselling and supported his self-referral to Barnabas House.

David had become unwell by the time I first saw him, and had not worked for six months. Existing on half pay, he was anxious about his future job security. He felt guilty and confused and kept asking me how, as an academic and a Christian, he could be this depressed and have so many problems. His church sympathised to a degree, but David looked reasonably fit, still attended Sunday services and church prayer meetings and, because of his jovial nature, appeared fairly normal in casual conversation.

When someone's face is covered with a measles rash or his leg is in plaster, most of us sympathise and ask if we can help, but when the affliction is invisible, it is harder to feel compassion. On the inside David felt confused, broken, lost and unable to cope. He could not read his Bible or even pray sometimes and he lay awake through many nights. He had been such a popular, capable, outgoing man – always laughing and joking. His family struggled as he transformed before their eyes into an introvert who found it a major struggle to step outside his own front door.

David and I met and planned two counselling sessions a week over a six-month period. We also worked with his wife and family where appropriate. It soon became obvious that David had to make an important decision about whether to give up work. His wife felt unable to cope with the thought, even though the family would have managed without serious financial difficulties. His church and fellow professionals could see little wrong and so put him under pressure not to resign. David knew that he would lose status in both spheres if he did hand in his notice, but he needed to give himself permission to rest; to realise that problems do happen to some, regardless of their faith or professionalism. He needed to see that his depression was not his fault, nor a sign of failure or inadequacy. He needed to explore every area of his life and to feel free to discuss any aspect of it.

David was on a high dose of medication and felt guilty about that too. We were working very closely with his doctor, who gradually lowered the dose as counselling progressed and David began to feel more relaxed. After some time, the pills were no longer necessary. David then felt that he wanted to spend hours reading the word of God and praying. Though I respected his good intentions in this, I sensed that at another level he was using a stock Christian response to hide from some real issues. After a few weeks he decided to face up to the position he was really in. For the first time in his life he talked about some of the root causes of his problems with a Christian who accepted him unconditionally.

He has commented since, 'For many weeks my counsellor and I sat in silence. I found it beneficial to be in such a special, safe place where I had time to look at my home, family and church situations.'

As he progressed through counselling we were able to spend time in prayer and in reading Scripture. I gave him some good, non-judgemental Christian material to read. He then made the decision to take early retirement from work and went on to become a part-time university lecturer and a teacher in his church. After completing a three-year course in counselling, David now counsels others in the area of depression. His doctor has expressed delight that he made such an excellent recovery.

I firmly believe that the church is a perfect place for finding restoration, peace and wholeness. With certain reservations I would say that it forms a safe refuge within our society. Per capita, more marriages survive and prosper within churches in this country than they do in the wider community (though that is no longer true in the USA). Many individuals find a relationship with God which releases them from the negative power of certain issues in their lives. I am aware of churches and other Christian organisations which do a wonderful work and see hundreds of damaged people come to wholeness. Others have a long way to go, and I have been deeply grieved that even today there is no meaningful system within many churches to facilitate honest communication and listening. If Christians do not offer this, people will turn to New Age organisations, and who can blame them? They extend compassion and consistency, impose no conditions and hold no expectancy of the people who come to them for help.

Christians need to address this problem. Ideally, I would love to see each local church with a team of trained counsellors. They would be as much built into its structure as the Sunday school or outreach team, for counsellors have the time and skills to support people with really serious problems in more depth than the pastoral and leadership teams ever can.

Some people in the church feel threatened by counselling

Progress is hampered because the whole idea of counselling, which encourages honest communication, can seem a real threat to many. They fear that it will open up a whole can of worms.

Reluctance to face the truth

I am appalled by what can go on behind closed doors in that secret place – the respectable, middle-class, and yes, sometimes Christian home. Police statistics show that more acts of violence, more murders, occur in ordinary homes at a weekend than on the streets of our roughest cities – except in the case of a major act of terrorism.

When the church preaches against the deadly sins on Sunday mornings it likes to see itself as more righteous than the world. Should any problems occur, both church leadership and individual Christians tend to cover them up and retire under a cloak of secrecy. Despite the new honesty of some, we fear that if we admit to our problems or sins, we will let down first God, then the church, our families and ourselves.

Christians cannot hope to find their way through the difficult maze of life if they shut their eyes and pretend that it does not exist. That is the way to bump into walls or obstacles and get hurt. We shut people in with their problems when we are reluctant to admit that such terrible things as the sexual abuse of children, or wife beating, can take place within the church family.

Many people will be shocked to learn that, at present, Barnabas House has an average of eighteen referrals a week resulting from situations where serious or ongoing violence has been shown towards women or children. Most of the perpetrators come from within the church. Of course, because of the nature of the Christian and professional service we offer, we see many of the worst cases. Most Christians – indeed most people – do not hit their wives or abuse children.

Still, it seems that never a week goes by when the media do not expose cases of Christians' involvement in abuse and other serious crimes. This makes us more than uncomfortable. We don't want to know. It is not simply that we loathe the gloating attitude of the tabloids. Christians faced up with the truth by counselling services or other professionals can also feel threatened. Many either dispute the facts aggressively or blame it all on the devil, hide behind a quick prayer and run away.

The facts are grim but verifiable. Court cases and statistics prove that every serious problem which occurs outside the church also occurs within it, and that includes the evangelical and charismatic end of the spectrum. Christian solicitors from all around the country regularly contact my organisation for help and support as they deal with Christian clients who are perpetrators of crime, as well as others who are victims.

Christians are not always the easiest people to counsel

Becoming a Christian can sometimes appear to add to people's problems, though of course the real culprit is not Christianity, but a false understanding of it. For example, non-religious managers who find themselves under severe stress at work will often take early retirement, but many Christian men and women have picked up such a strong work ethic that they feel guilty about this remedy. Instead they continue slaving away until they have a nervous breakdown or a heart attack.

Sadly, Christians who are depressed often seek help far too late, because they feel so guilty. As a general rule, the earlier someone with depression talks about it, the quicker they will recover. I am delighted that there has been an increase in the provision of good Christian counselling for those suffering from depression, but counsellors will not be able to do much good if Christians are reluctant to make use of their services.

I have to say as well that we are more successful at counselling in the area of marriage with non church-goers than with Christians. The former are not afraid to express strong emotions such as hatred. When they shout and swear at each other at least they are being real and we have something to work on. The Christians, in trying to appear 'good', bottle up the hurt of years. It poisons everything with a deep bitterness which makes problems far less easy to resolve.

The answer in all these situations is not running away from counselling at one extreme or blaming God at the other, but for Christians to come alongside, to educate, train and bring some truth and light into the situation.

Christians can fail to rescue their own

I have noticed in all sorts of spheres that people shy away from helping others in difficulty if they see those people as different from themselves. Perhaps they feel unable to cope with another's pain. This was exactly the way I felt when I first started working with people with physical disabilities. Only by actually getting to know them did I lose that fear, and it is the same with anyone who is hurting emotionally. Surely Jesus' love can help us here, and yet many churches blithely pray, 'God's kingdom come,' when they are not prepared to help damaged Christians, let alone the wider community.

I accept that some Christian organisations will never see counselling as part of their role. That is fine, provided they are prepared to refer people on to appropriate sources of help, and are supportive. Too often, however, they appear anxious when we talk about raising standards in counselling in terms of keeping logs, establishing codes of practice, etc. It is almost as though they feel that good counselling practice threatens their own viability as caring pastors.

I am particularly concerned about the number of church leaders we see who have struggled under overwhelming pressures for years. Those who break silence can, in certain circumstances, face losing everything. For example, several ministers have, of their own volition, informed their church organisations that they are practising homosexuals. No longer willing to live a lie, these men were looking for help, yet immediately they said anything they were suspended or sacked, losing job, house, church, relationships and the considerable respectability and status they once enjoyed. Some have told me that they felt their problems dated back to times when they were abused as children, yet their church or house-church structures offered little or no support. With marriage and family plunged into crisis, made worse by their sudden loss of income, these men were left feeling guilt-ridden and isolated. Several have had nervous breakdowns.

The church's knee-jerk reaction of shock–horror–rejection will solve nothing. They might not feel able to condone what someone has done, but they could consider building into their infrastructures mechanisms to help and support their former servants who are working through difficult issues. It ought to go without saying that they should do the same for their families.

The need for training

I am more convinced than ever of the need for Christians to be involved in restoring and helping their own. Due largely to ignorance and lack of understanding, some secular counsellors can be aggressive towards Christian values – as David found. That is why it is essential that committed Christians who are badly hurt have the opportunity to receive help from a Christian base, if they wish. However, there is a huge need for training and a raising of standards and awareness among Christian counsellors and carers. Their service has to be every bit as professional as that offered by the best secular counselling.

Once Christians start being honest about difficult or persistent problems or sin, their churches realise that they need people equipped to help. For example, they may not know by instinct how to counsel a woman who reveals that she was badly abused as a child, a couple whose adopted teenage son is in trouble with the police, or a man who survives an accident in which his wife and baby are killed. Also, even when operating only within their own churches, Christians cannot act outside of the law and many are realising that they need to keep abreast of changes, such as the implications of the new Community Care and Children Acts.

Progress

I feel very encouraged about the number of churches that are asking for training, support and help in order to build their own counselling teams. Many major Christian organisations are now asking for a complete programme of training lasting for not a few months but two or three years. Christians should be at the forefront of setting high standards of wise care, as we have already seen demonstrated in organisations such as ACET (AIDS Care, Education and Training), CARE and the Evangelical Alliance.

Others have recognised the skills which already exist within their church, whether parenting, pastoring and teaching or professional ones such as medical or social work. These churches sometimes ask for further training because they feel that God has called them to reach out into their community to extend Christ's gospel ministry of binding up the broken-hearted, comforting those who mourn, proclaiming freedom for the captives and release from darkness for the prisoners.

We are now seeing Christians involved in local church-run centres which cater for single mothers, alcoholics, the homeless or the unemployed in their communities. Christians may be running medical practices, retreat centres or offering residential or day counselling. Individuals are also involved in hospices and mental health facilities. By the next century I foresee a network of such centres throughout the country – all linked together, sharing resources and expertise and working with the highest standards of training and practice.

But what form of counselling? What training?

The minds of human beings are so highly complex that learned professors and psychologists spend a lifetime studying them, without ever coming to an end. Our emotions, bodies, spirits, imagination, genetic make-up and varied experiences – and the way these react together – make a whole maze in themselves, to say nothing of the way we all fit together in society. This may explain why there are so many different approaches to counselling and psychotherapy, often contradicting each other but all claiming to be therapeutic.

I undertook a training in secular counselling methods which lasted for over five years. In the mornings we learned about some non-directive methods, and in the afternoons we studied some directive ones. As these opposed each other's methodologies and theories and had little ground in common, we students had to make sure that we gave the right essay in to the right person, or we would get terrible marks! There are various schools, including the behaviourists, psychoanalysts, personalists and transpersonalists, and all of these exist in many different forms. Then there are those who follow the newer therapies such as Gestalt or Transactional Analysis. This book is not the place to explore these methods and theories. Roger Hurding describes and then analyses them from a Christian viewpoint in his excellent book *Roots and Shoots*.

Christian or secular training?

To make matters more complicated, no one defined theory and methodology called 'Christian counselling' exists either. However, we do have Christian counsellors, and they should not be surprised by the fact that they sometimes see things differently from each other. The Bible says that only God is big enough to understand and know each individual completely: 'Such knowledge [about myself] is too wonderful for me, too lofty for me to attain' (Psalm 139:6). Each of us, as we try to help others, can only hope to grasp some of the truth about human nature and the way people work.

There is further debate among Christians as to whether counselling should be based on the Bible only, secular theories only or a mixture (see Chapter 6 for further reading on this subject). Parts of secular theories are acceptable to most Christians; other parts seem to go against a biblical view of man and the world. Should Christian counsellors only take into account truth found within Scripture, or can they draw on the sometimes very useful insights of man? I would tend to take an eclectic view, drawing from the secular models of Rogers, Egan and others, but avoiding anything within them which conflicts with Christian ethics or worldview. I also seek help from Scripture, prayer and the Holy Spirit. I would expect a Christian counsellor to work according to biblical assumptions, aims and methods, practised within a framework of Christian commitment, insight and values.

However, some Christians, in embracing secular methods with enthusiasm, have strayed into a form of syncretism, where alien beliefs are merged with the tenets of mainstream Christianity. This carries the danger of Christian clients being misled – into New Age practices, for example. Worried about this, some Christians dismiss counselling altogether. Therefore it is important for Christians who counsel other Christians to have a clearly stated basis of faith, and to practise in the light of it.

It is also a fact that the wider community can be suspicious of evangelical Christians working in the field of counselling or other forms of social care. A non-Christian sociologist once said to me that today's society would never have allowed Dr Barnado or the founders of the National Children's Home to begin their work, simply because they were active Christians. One Local Authority offered our organisation a large grant if we would take the word 'Christian' out of our literature. As that would have meant working under false pretences, we refused – and lost the grant.

We live in a multi-cultural society and one of the major challenges to the Christian church in this generation is to be able to offer an excellent standard of care to all in the community who wish to use it. In this must be 'harmless as doves' and not operate under any hidden agendas. Occasionally Christian counsellors shoot themselves in the foot by abusing their position, for example by trying to push their own beliefs with their clients, or by failing to work in co-operation with the law, the medical profession, etc.

We must also be 'wise as serpents'. Those counsellors whose training comes solely from certain Christian models will tend to be more directive in their approach to clients than would many secular norms. This may cause conflicts which further training might resolve. If we expect Social Service departments or other agencies to make referrals to us, we will have to offer standards which equal or exceed those which would be found in hospitals or other professional bodies.

It is vital to establish signpost standards in the maze in order to protect the best interests of all clients and to prevent further unnecessary suspicion between the secular and Christian worlds.

Barnabas House and its related organisations offer similar professional services to those found in the secular community, covering all major areas of family work, child abuse, finance, stress, depression, bereavement, trauma and disaster. All our counsellors and staff are fully trained in these areas and work under a code of ethics and practice. We give all clients full information before we begin any work with them, making it clear that we are a Christian counselling and caring organisation. Trustees govern us, and other outside assessors check our work on a regular basis. All this has meant that our service has been taken up by many Social Service, probation and health-care departments which refer people on to us. Over the years we have established a good relationship of trust with those organisations.

What is God's attitude and agenda in all of this?

In the midst of all the confusion the Christian counsellor has to try to understand what is God's attitude – not only to the client who asks God for help, but to the one who does not acknowledge him at all. I believe that God made us. He understands and cares about every aspect of people's lives. Jesus fed the hungry and ministered to the community around, whether they followed him or not. The Bible gives a great cry for social justice and asks us to fight on behalf of the poor and those with no voice. It also emphasises the responsibility of all individuals to do as they would be done by and certainly not to cause others pain. God is passionately concerned about those kinds of things, which are quite compatible with most secular counselling. Of course he also longs that everyone should know him, but he will never force people into a relationship with himself.

The real distinctive of a Christian counsellor is that he will be God-centred rather than person-centred, and will bring his clients to the heart of Father God in prayer. We have hope because, in one sense, God is like the man who sits on a platform high above the maze and can direct any who are lost and ask for his help. Not for nothing is his Holy Spirit called the Counsellor, the Advocate, the Comforter, the one who draws alongside.

We have to accept, however, that many who seek our help will not necessarily become Christians – nor should it be part of our main aim and objectives that they do so.

I have seen too many Welsh hell-fire preachers scare people into deciding to become Christians before they are ready. Often those who make commitments in this way later go back on them. On the other hand I believe that the Holy Spirit sometimes helps non-believers at least begin to find their way towards himself through the Christian counsellor's genuine care and quiet prayer, even when God and the Bible are never mentioned at all. I have seen it happen.

For example, one man was referred to me by his solicitor. A docker and ex-boxer, Steve was six foot six and married to a tiny wife. Some time previously he had broken her jaw and his marriage was in a mess. He had consulted his solicitor about a divorce.

The first thing Steve said to me when he came in the door was, 'I'm only here because my solicitor sent me. I've no time for religion and I don't want to know anything about God!'

'Fine!' I said. 'I've no problem with that.' We arranged a series of six counselling sessions, during which some remarkable work was done. The couple discovered that they did love each other and, after working through various issues, cancelled their divorce. This meant that their solicitor lost a lot of money!

Eight months later Steve phoned me. 'I wanted to tell you that we're still doing fine. In fact we've both become Christians and we're going to the local church. God has really blessed our lives through you!'

'But I never mentioned God to you once!' I exclaimed.

'I know, and I want to thank you for that. I was testing you out.'

I remembered that he had tried to goad me into talking about God several times, but I had felt strongly that it was not an appropriate time or place and that I should leave the Holy Spirit to do his work.

Steve commented that he had seen something in the service we offered. 'You could have ripped me off, but you made no charge at all,' he said. In fact he had sent us a generous gift.

Obviously I was delighted that this couple had found God, but I am still convinced that the role of a Christian counsellor is to show compassion, not to preach. If Steve and his wife had not become Christians at that time, we would have still fulfilled our purpose by showing them care and helping them find healing in themselves and in their relationship. God is interested in those things too.

6

Christians in Counselling

What makes a good Christian counsellor?

A counsellor who is lost in his own maze of inner conflicts and turmoil will only confuse the issue for his clients. He must know and understand himself, or he may project some of his own problems onto his client. For example, if he has taken up counselling because he is lonely himself and has never resolved that state of affairs, then he may become dependent on clients. Also, the kind of person who is always judging others can wreak havoc in counselling. We have to accept people as they are, without immediately looking for or guaranteeing change, and some Christians find this hard.

If someone is to become an effective counsellor, before he even thinks about gaining knowledge and techniques, he will need certain qualities. Secular counselling theory acknowledges that the personality and character of the therapist are more effective in helping the client than the method used. In their book *Towards Effective Counselling and Psychotherapy: training and practice* (Aldine, 1967) Charles Truax and Robert Carkhuff define the three qualities essential to a counsellor as:

  1. Genuineness (being in touch with one's own feelings);

What makes a good counsellor?

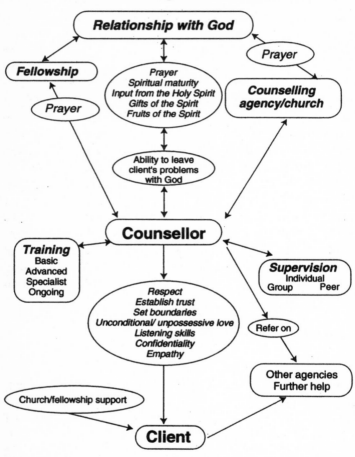

2. Non-possessive warmth (or unconditional regard for the person, even if one does not like what he has done);

3. Accurate empathy (or the ability to come alongside and understand how the client is feeling).

These qualities, by another name, could equate to some of the fruits of the Spirit. God can help an individual to grow them.

There is so much I could say on this subject, but perhaps it is best expressed by the story of my wife's inward journey. I owe a great deal to Glenys. I could never have managed what amounted to in effect several jobs at once, had she not supported me at home. In addition, she has always liked helping people – that is why she became a nurse – but, all through the years, I knew that there was more in her than the quiet coper everyone saw.

Glenys used to be held back by a narrow religious upbringing. She tended to see everything as black or white, but she changed after God went to work on her attitudes, enabling her to become such an effective counsellor that she now heads up that side of our work at Barnabas House. She also leads some of our training courses, and whenever she talks about the journey on which she has come, she gives heart to those who feel that they would never make good counsellors. I think it will be best, though, if she tells her own story.

Glenys' story

I was born just after the war, the youngest of five children, and we enjoyed a happy enough childhood. We attended church and Sunday school as a family, but at the age of twelve I decided that I wanted to know Jesus for myself. From then on my faith never altered, although there have been times when I followed Jesus more closely than at others!

My parents were quiet and strict. Looking back, I'm not sure that I was ever quite myself at home. I'm an outgoing person really, but the rest of the family were very reserved. Sometimes they accused me of showing off. If I was to fit into the family and be seen as good, I learned that I should serve others quietly, then melt into the background.

I must have learned the lesson quickly for, right from my early days at school, if a teacher wanted someone to run an errand she would say, 'I'll send Glenys, she's so capable!' I felt I had to live up to that image – capable, helpful, always doing the right thing. I was terribly grown-up as a child.

Later on at school I was the kind of person everyone comes to with their problems. Being fairly logical, with a good measure of common sense, I always had an answer ready, but if anyone failed to follow my advice, woe betide them! I never noticed when people backed away, not wanting to open up their hearts to a little answer-giving machine.

My grandparents had been real 'Holy Roller' Christians as a result of the famous Welsh Revival of the early years of this century, but sadly, over the years, their vibrant experience of God had hardened into rigid rule-keeping. The females in our family could never wear trousers or ear-rings and other ornaments. I remember having my hair cut urchin-style at the age of twelve. The next time I visited Gran she spoke softly, referring to Scripture, 'A woman's hair is her glory, Glen!' I felt weighed down by guilt until it grew long again. After I became a Christian I adopted a different set of rules, believing that it was incumbent on me to think and eat and dress like an Elim Pentecostal.

Later, Roger found it hard when I tried to impose rules and regulations on our own children, for he had been brought up in a much more free and easy environment. By and large, though, I played the submissive wife. I cooked and cleaned and looked after everybody, keeping extremely busy – which made me appear godly and stopped me thinking too deeply. I attended church meetings three times on Sundays and twice in the week, but never played a very active role – not many women did in those days.

All this time I grew very little, spiritually. Elim Pentecostals spoke in tongues, which 'proved' that they were specially blessed by God. No one in Elim had an excuse for struggling with sin or problems – ever. Or so I believed! If someone broke the outward code of behaviour, I would tend to be far harder on them than God ever was. I saw everything in terms of black and white, shoulds and shouldn'ts, and generally felt it was my responsibility to tidy up people's lives.

When a new minister came in the early 1970s and tried to introduce earth-shattering new ideas such as moving the pews, I had a few things to say. When he suggested that people might dance in church . . . well, that was too much. We upped and left! Yet despite this, I managed to think of myself as quite flexible and open-minded.

Shortly after that we moved to Carmarthen, where I continued to go to church, but I can remember feeling a kind of creeping desperation. A few times I cried out, 'What's wrong with me? I want to be more alive in you, Lord!' Yet I needed to feel very much in control. I could not abide any form of charismatic worship, for example. If upstart church denominations wanted to speak in tongues all of a sudden, I felt that they should join Elim, which had everything neat and in order.

When Roger began counselling in our house, I spoke politely to the people who came, for I was a very nice person who never failed to do the right thing. Afterwards, however, I would complain, 'For goodness sake, Roger, how much longer are you going to listen to those people rabbiting on about themselves, week in, week out? What's

the point? If they got on their knees before the Lord,
they'd soon be sorted out!'

'It's not that simple, Glen,' Roger objected.

'People never had all these problems in Elim!'

'Didn't they?'

'Of course not. With the Lord and the Holy Spirit –
well, we're new creations, aren't we now?' I said, smugly.

'So feeling hurt would let the side down, would it?'

'Well, the Bible says we should rejoice in the Lord!'

It was not until we started meeting with the Carmarthen
Christian Fellowship that God started to chip away at
some of my wrong thinking. In that environment I could
grow spiritually at last. Suddenly I saw that Christianity
was concerned not with a series of do's and don'ts, but
with Jesus' love for me and mine for him; with a relationship of faith and not a desperate clinging to self-
righteousness. Furthermore, God was big enough to look
after himself and had no need of my help in judging others
and sorting out all their problems for them.

The story of the woman at the well came alive for me
(John 4:1–26). I realised that although Jesus talked
straight to this woman who had so many 'husbands', he
never condemned her. Stepping right outside cultural
prohibitions, he treated her with respect as a human being
and was more than willing to relate to her – not after she
changed her ways, but before. He loved unconditionally,
and saw value in everyone.

Individuals in the fellowship had come from a number
of different denominations, but as we grew to respect
and love one another, slowly many of our prejudices
broke down. God began to de-programme me and, after
two years, I no longer felt guilty if I did not eat and
dress and talk like an Elim Pentecostal. I realised that I
could be myself. How wonderful! Maybe I didn't have to
melt into the background; maybe I had a part to play.
Roger had been telling me this and affirming me for

years, but because I had no sense of inner well-being, I had never really listened.

He encouraged me to sit in on some of his counselling sessions, where I kept my mouth firmly shut. Afterwards, I would sometimes venture, 'Why didn't you ask so and so, Roger?'

'Brilliant idea! I'd never have thought of that!'

Soon Roger urged me to take more of a lead. I'd had no training and at first there were times when he threw up his hands in horror. I asked one client a slightly foolish question – had she enjoyed a normal childhood?

'Oh yes,' the woman replied with great enthusiasm, and then went on to describe how her parents had had her working as a prostitute at the age of eight.

'Look, love,' I said, leaning across to her, 'if anyone asks you if you had a normal childhood again, the answer's "no", right!'

The woman's face fell, her illusions shattered. But even from my mistakes I began to learn something of the value of letting people talk, of giving them space to do things their way and not coming up with instant solutions to their problems. For unless people see something for themselves, they are unlikely to change.

I began to sit in on every session where Roger counselled a woman, and sometimes when he counselled a man, if he felt a female viewpoint would add something to that particular situation. I don't know if I helped anyone very much at this stage, but God was certainly using these times to change me! One of our first residential clients was telling us how she had been abused as a child. In doing so she became quite distressed.

'Would you like me to sit with you?' I asked.

The woman, Angela, nodded through her sobs and so I sat beside her on the sofa, putting my arm around her. Angela calmed enough to begin talking again – about a relationship with a woman friend, which had become a

full-blown lesbian affair. I had always reacted in a judgemental way at the mere mention of the word 'lesbian'. I
felt myself go stiff, and I started a silent conversation with
the Lord: 'Dear Jesus, what are you *doing* to me? I'm
sitting here with this woman in my arms! Her head's on
my chest!'

'What are you afraid of, Glen?' the Lord seemed to say
in reply. 'She's not going to hurt you. She has a broken
heart!'

The narrow framework in which I lived was widening
by the minute.

In those early days God was dealing with me through so
many incidents. Chapter 3 tells the story of how a con-
man deceived me on my very first day in full-time counselling. Afterwards I kept moaning to anyone who would
listen, 'If I see him in Tescos I'll shop him for sure!'
Though normally calm and level-headed, I seethed with
fury for two months. Looking back, I realise that God was
teaching me more about myself – in particular that I could
get angry.

Now I can laugh at my mistakes, as eventually I did
over that con-man. I have also found it important to learn
from them that we should presume nothing but check all
things. I remember we matrons in the training college kept
hearing noises coming from the room above where we
worked – day after day and night after night. The room
was occupied by a male student and we became convinced
that the regular thumpings and sounds of heavy breathing
meant that he had a young lady with him.

Eventually we decided to obtain a pass key and
investigate. We burst into the room only to discover
the student sitting on a rowing machine. I will never
forget the look of surprise on his sweat-covered face
because several matrons had suddenly burst through his
door. We could only mutter a quick 'sorry' and make a
hasty exit!

Coming up to date, when I take one of our training courses, I see the students sitting there, tense and worried, or maybe feeling a little inadequate on their first day. I start by telling them some of the stories you have just read, and watch them begin to relax. Hopefully they glimpse something of the way I used to be. If *I* could change and become an effective counsellor with God's help then anyone can! We're all on a journey. Unless a counsellor first knows himself and then learns how to grow and change, how can he expect his clients to do the same? Unless a counsellor knows his own limitations, he may neglect to refer his client on, should it become necessary.

So many of the principles of being a good counsellor are summed up in Jesus' words, 'Do to others what you would have them do to you' (Matthew 7:12). Since I have stopped seeing everything in terms of black and white, I have found it so much easier to identify with clients. I know, for example, that if I had to travel all the way to Inverness to tell some unknown woman my problems, I'd be a nervous wreck. So during the first couple of sessions I work on establishing trust, making sure the client knows that whatever she tells me I will still accept her as a person, and that I will not spill the beans, even in the guise of a prayer request. Sadly, churches often 'leak', so it is important that clients understand that what they say to the counsellor is confidential within certain limits which are clearly defined.

It is also important that she knows I have heard her, so I will reflect back some of what she says and also make sure that I remember vital details by taking notes and going through them before the next session. Again, so that she does not worry about leaks of information, it is important that the client knows what will happen to those notes. Often I will hand them to her at the end of the series of sessions.

If I can mention some small thing not directly associated with the counselling, it helps the client to understand that I see her as a person, not a problem. So, if she has told me that she has to rush off to take her dog to the vet, next session I might ask how the animal is.

Also I make sure that she knows the boundaries, so that she does not become wrongly dependent on me. From my own point of view, and that of my family, it is vital that I do not carry my clients' problems around with me all the time. At the end of the day I have to let them go, and I am so grateful that I can leave them with God. Counsellors who take on a wrong sense of responsibility for sorting everything out, will start to suffer from stress themselves or maybe run the danger of co-dependency. That means that they need the client as much as the other way round – a mutually destructive relationship where no growth is possible.

Most of the time, as a counsellor, I feel that I am accompanying my client a little way on her journey. I hope that as I draw alongside, she may glimpse a ray of hope, and see that things will change, in time. I am still learning, and hope I always will. For example, I have put my arm around a bereaved person and said, 'There, there. I understand!' I thought I did! Until my dad died, though, I had no idea what the wail felt like. It took time to come through that experience, but I have learned and grown through it. No one can take that away from me. I am not the same person I was before.

Sometimes it can be helpful for all of us to look back and see where we have come from. Speaking for myself, it always makes me thankful.

Pastoral and community counselling

Pastoral counselling takes place within the church, and community counselling outside of it. Barnabas House

was one of the first organisations within the broadly
evangelical wing of the church to counsel in both
fields, though others have followed since. Of course
many individual Christians counsel in the wider community – for example those attached to doctors' surgeries,
secular counselling agencies or those within professions
such as medical or social work, the emergency services
and armed forces.

Though counselling can form an important part of the
church's ministry to its own members and perhaps to the
wider community, it should never take over the whole
work of the church. The Bible makes it clear that all
Christians are called to encourage and build one another
up. On top of that, some will be called to teach or to pastor
or to counsel, but not all Christians are called to be
counsellors. Those who are will form quite a narrow
band within the church, as will those who need their
services.

What are Christian counsellors?

Quite simply, Christian counsellors are counsellors who
are Christians. I do not believe that there is any one thing
called Christian counselling. There are almost as many
methods as there are counsellors. However, as I have said,
secular research has shown that the personality and attitude of the counsellor (showing unconditional, unposses-
sive love, for example) are of more importance in bringing
positive results than the exact method used.

If we believe in a God who reveals himself through the
Bible, through Jesus and the Holy Spirit, then these things
will shape our whole worldview, especially our understanding of the nature and make-up of man, which will
in turn affect the way we see our clients.

Christians believe that man was created by God in his
own image to have a special relationship with him. How-

ever, because sin came into the world, he has fallen from grace, and the loving relationship for which he was made can only be restored through the cross of Jesus. It is clear that man is not all evil, but he can easily be captured by sin, which includes selfish or wrong ways of thinking, as well as obvious crimes like murder. The New Testament tells how Jesus came to set the captives free, but this will only happen when a person comes to know and trust him. The first commandment is the key to the way forward: ' "Love the Lord your God with all your heart and with all your soul and with all your strength and with all your mind"; and, "Love your neighbour as yourself" ' (Luke 10:27). If people followed this, everything else would fall into place.

If Christian counsellors work in a pastoral setting, our clients may share perspectives similar to those outlined above. Clients from the wider community may hold a different worldview. Christians can still counsel them productively, using secular models, but these have certain weaknesses. One problem with person-centred counselling, for example, is that it tends to assume that man is basically good and only needs the best in him drawing out. Many people find that the task of trying to change themselves from within is simply too great, so person-centred counselling can only take them a certain distance.

Some other schools of counselling and psychotherapy take the view that man is full of problems and destructive drives and the best he can hope for is to accommodate some of the worst ones through constant therapy. This can lead to the self-indulgent 'therapeutic society' which we see among better-off Americans.

The people I meet never seem to be wholly good or wholly bad. Most of us are neither Hitlers nor Mother Teresas. If we are honest, we will acknowledge that we can be kind one minute and selfish the next, and that there are parts of ourselves that we don't like. The Judeo/ Christian view of man seems to me to fit the evidence of what I see. Man, as God's highest creation, can be very, very good, but sin has spoiled things and now he is capable of great evil also. Christianity says that we don't have to spiral downwards, despite the evil within us or the evil and hurt which may be inflicted upon us by others. Help is available through the cross and resurrection of Jesus. Christian counsellors can be full of both hope and realism.

Secular methods as used by Christians

Many purely Christian methods of counselling are far too directive for the secular world to stomach. This can be a problem if those trained and accredited in the Christian side want to counsel in a broader field. I myself was trained in secular models and will draw from several of them when counselling in both pastoral and community settings. Mainly I use methods of non-directive or person-centred counselling. I am fairly happy with these as far as they go, though no one has ever produced any concrete evidence that they work!

One danger with Christian clients is that they hide behind familiar Bible verses or a prayer, and fail to listen. That is why, for the first few sessions even with Christians, I normally use a secular, person-centred approach. It tends to result in them being more real about themselves. Many have said afterwards that they appreciated talking to someone 'normal' who didn't throw scriptures at them, make them feel that they had failed God or try to 'pray away' their problem.

In crisis situations I will use secular methods of directive or intervention counselling. This would be where I feared that a client might harm himself or others, or where for some other reason he was temporarily incapable of making his own decisions. Some secular counsellors would do the same, though not all would agree that a counsellor should, under any circumstances, take on responsibility for his client.

Christians may choose different methods from the huge array of secular therapies available. There are a number of good models, though we may find many lacking in terms of their value bases. Christians have the advantage of being able to refer to a final authority among the bewildering variety of possible ideas and approaches. In this maze of conflicting theories, among the confusion of a million branching passageways, the Bible provides signposts. Provided that methods are not in conflict with the basics of Christian faith or ethics as defined in Scripture, they may give helpful insights into the complex way in which people's minds or emotions work.

Does a Christian counsellor offer something extra?

Christians believe that any problem can be taken to the heart of Father God. If I am counselling other Christians, at the end of the session we can pray and seek God's guidance together. I may use the Bible which, in the maze of an individual's or family's problems, provides firm reference points and the kind of truth which sets people free.

I can deal directly with spiritual issues in a Christian client's life, because we share the belief that the spiritual element of humanity is important – a view which is hotly contested by some secular counsellors. Obviously, even sympathetic non-believing counsellors will be less effective in helping Christians to develop their spiritual side.

Unlike those who do not believe in anything outside of themselves, a Christian client does not have to depend solely on finding his own inner resources. Neither does he need to depend on changing his environment or on endless counselling sessions. Christian counsellors have a much wider scope to work in than their secular counterparts because we can invite the Holy Spirit to help. Real change and growth can take place. For this reason I believe that counselling between Christians does not need to continue indefinitely, as many secular therapies are inclined to do.

Another distinctive of Christian counsellors is our aim. So far as Christian clients are concerned this may be to help them grow in their faith and become more Christlike, rather than simply to become more whole and self-fulfilled. Even if someone's tough circumstances never change, even if their emotional wounds are never fully healed, they can still find acceptance and purpose in Jesus. Christians can take responsibility for some of the sinful attitudes which do them real harm – such as bitterness, jealousy or hatred – and ask the Holy Spirit to help them change from the inside.

When working in the wider community, unless the client expressly asks for Christian input, we have a professional code of conduct which ensures that we counsel without mentioning God or seeking to influence our client's worldview. Some 20% of our referrals at Barnabas House come from doctors, Social Services, health-care departments, etc. They are fully aware that we are a Christian organisation, but they also know that our main aim is not evangelism and that we are not about to abuse their trust by forcing our beliefs down anyone's throat.

Not all clients come through referrals. Individuals from the wider community sometimes seek out Christian counsellors because they feel that the added dimension of God's help is on offer. In our multi-faith society they have a right to do this under the Community Care Act, provided that the counsellor is accredited with an appropriate organisation.

We use humanistic person-centred methods, in the same way as a secular counselling agency, to give clients a safe setting in which to explore their pain. Though the counsellor himself is God-centred, we are not actively seeking to bring our clients to faith, for it is not our place to do any converting. We are happy to leave that to God, and I am astounded at how many clients do subsequently come to know Jesus for themselves — more than ever did through our efforts at evangelism in the various churches I pastored!

Prayer is a key. Perhaps the most important thing we do is to bring all clients to the heart of Father God in prayer, before they come and after they leave. I will also be praying during the session, but not out loud! Prayer involves listening as well as speaking. As well as helping the client directly, I believe that sometimes God helps me as a counsellor to see my way forward.

The team meets for prayer regularly. We also send a fortnightly prayer letter to a team of intercessors who are based all around the country. In it we list our practical needs and also might mention, for example, that there is one situation where we feel a little stuck. We give no specific details, but they pray. God knows, and somehow things start to happen!

'Mr Jones' was a striking example of prayer at work. He had no religious beliefs himself, but his employers sent him to us because he had asked for counselling from Christians. I began the session by using Carl Rogers' models of non-directive, person-centred counselling, but it seemed hard going so I tried some other approaches which my secular training had taught me.

Halfway through the first interview the client interrupted me, 'We're not getting anywhere, are we, Mr Altman?'

Inwardly I agreed with what he said, but, following my training, I reflected his statement back. 'You feel we're not moving on at all?'

'Quite. But you're a Christian. Don't you think we could pray about this?'

I came alongside him to pray for a moment, but had not said six words when he suddenly exclaimed, 'I've got it!' With that he stood up and strode out.

What had he got? I felt decidedly worried. We had covered so little ground in the session. For all I knew he might have been suffering from severe depression and be rushing off to commit suicide. I talked with my supervisor, but as we were unsuccessful in renewing contact with Mr Jones, there was little we could do – except pray.

A few months later I saw him coming out of a church building with his wife and teenage daughter. He came across the road to talk to me and explained that he had been working abroad.

'But I've been wanting to thank you!' he said. 'When you prayed I knew exactly what I needed to do!'

That was more than I did! I thought. Whatever had I prayed in those few words?

'I knew that I needed to sort some things out with my wife,' Mr Jones continued. 'When I did I felt a great cloud of pain and guilt lift off me. And we started going to church, thanks to you. My daughter became a Christian this morning!'

I had said nothing about God, preached nothing, prayed virtually nothing in Mr Jones' presence. Later I counselled him about some other issues, and I can say that he is a changed man.

This kind of thing does not happen every day, but secular theory would be wrong to say that it does not happen at all. Contrary to much current thinking in counselling circles, I feel that we must allow people to grow and develop the spiritual side of themselves. Whether overtly or not, I hope that our work at Barnabas House is characterised by the help of the Holy Spirit, prayer and the unconditional, *agape* love which Jesus spoke of.

7

The Association of Christian Counsellors – Its History and Purpose

The problem

In 1988 my Local Authority sent me as its delegate to a large professional conference on counselling and care in the community. Looking around I saw representatives from many people groups, such as the gay, disabled and ethnic communities, but no one from the church, not even the Evangelical Alliance or CARE who usually attend such events. When it came time for questions from the floor I asked, 'Where is the church?'

'We put advertisements in the press, but no one came forward,' the chairman replied.

'Well, I'm here on behalf of my Local Authority, but would you mind if I represent the church as well?' I asked – and sensed the atmosphere turning slightly hostile. *Keep within your church buildings where you're no threat*, it seemed to say. *Don't get churches involved in the wider community, and don't mix your professional with your private life!*

Afterwards a senior civil servant approached me. 'Mr Altman,' he said, 'I wonder, could you do something with regard to the church?'

'What do you mean?' I replied.

'Well, something needs to be done about standards in

counselling. I see some Christian organisations producing so-called "trained counsellors" by the barrel-load. They go around asking for jobs in doctors' surgeries or other statutory agencies, but no one knows who these people are. What are their procedures, their codes of ethics? To whom are they accountable?'

'I see what you're saying. But what are you suggesting that *I* could do about it?'

'I was wondering if you could think about setting up some kind of umbrella organisation to provide accreditation and all the rest?'

Later I found out that this man was a Christian whose work gave him insight into the future direction of legislation on counselling in this country. His words started me thinking – and praying.

By 1990 more colleagues working in secular fields were telling me of their concern over Christians who were going to statutory bodies, saying that they were trained counsellors. In some cases they had damaged the clients they saw. Why did these Christians lack professional standards, I wondered? Why were they not properly trained or supervised? What was going wrong?

Why set up something separate and Christian when other accrediting organisations already exist?

Organisations such as the British Association for Counselling (BAC), the Association for Pastoral Care and Counselling and the Association of Psychotherapists set the highest standards in terms of accreditation, training, ethics and supervision in counselling. They do a wonderful work and we can learn a great deal from them. I saw, though, that many evangelical Christians believed that these organisations did not understand them; that they were antagonistic towards their worldview or that of their clients. Many felt unable to go along with some of the premises in training courses recommended by these organisations.

If evangelicals were not to 'throw the baby out with the bathwater', but rather to be encouraged to raise standards, perhaps they needed to do this through a new kind of organisation. It would have to be seen as acceptable both to themselves and to the secular world, and it would have to enable its accredited counsellors to keep the uniqueness of their Christian beliefs.

Thinking about these things, I could see the need for the kind of umbrella organisation which the civil servant had suggested. At first I believed that one of the respected organisations already in existence would best fulfil the role. The Evangelical Alliance, CARE and CWR, for example, all had some interest in counselling, but further enquiries showed me that none of them saw themselves in the role of a body which would regulate Christians in counselling. We needed something similar to the British Association of Counsellors, which would be acceptable in both church and community settings. Then it could set standards, accredit Christians who worked in counselling, advise on training programmes and supervision, and provide accountability, support and a number of other things.

How the ACC started

One Saturday in May 1990 I was sitting at home when a Dr Mervyn Suffield phoned. I knew that he came from an organisation called Christians in Caring Professions, but had previously spoken with him only once, for a few moments at a meeting.

'Roger, as I travel around the country I keep hearing about you,' Mervyn began. 'It seems we have similar interests. Could we meet?'

'Fine!' I said.

'Only I'm in Carmarthen now. I could be with you in twenty minutes!'

'Whereabouts are you, exactly?' I asked, thinking to give him directions.

'Under the big castle.'

'What kind of castle?' I asked, puzzled. The fortified ruins in our town are seldom described as large.

'Oh, you know, huge towers, moat – the place where the Prince of Wales was invested.'

'Mervyn,' I laughed, 'you've a bit of a problem. You're in Caernarfon, North Wales. We're in Carmarthen, West Wales. It's a three-hour journey – on a good day!'

He did not seem at all put out. 'See you early evening then!'

Sure enough he arrived, with his wife and three children. They stayed the night and as we talked I realised quickly that despite his abysmal knowledge of Welsh geography, this Englishman and I had much in common. We shared the same vision for establishing not only accountability in counselling, but also good standards and methods of working and training. I operated from a small base. It would have been hard for me to go to churches in the UK proposing to set up the kind of organisation I had in mind. 'Who are you?' they might have asked, with some justification. On the other hand Mervyn, with his position in CiCP, could bring people together much more easily.

We prayed that night and continued to meet on a regular basis in order to plan – usually in the less than peaceful surroundings of an M4 service station. I found Mervyn to be quite an innovator – a man of action as well as words. We decided to call a meeting in Reading, inviting various churches and para-church organisations to consider giving us a mandate to get our project underway.

In January 1991 every organisation we had invited to Reading turned up. They included CWR, Ellel Grange, CARE, YWAM, Bristol Network, CiCP – the list could go on and on. It turned out to be the first time they had all met together under one roof about anything! There and then they gave us the mandate to set up the organisation now known as the Association of Christian Counsellors.

One spin-off for me personally was the increased contact with others of stature who could influence my life. Ernest McQuoid from CARE, Bob Barham (a lecturer in social care and counselling who now runs his own consultancy and training agency), Gerald Coates from Pioneer, Steve Hepden (then from Bristol Christian Fellowship and now from Ellel Grange), Paul and Gretel Hagglin from the USA, Roger Hurding, formerly from Bristol University, who founded the Network Counselling Centre – all these and more brought helpful input to me personally, and to our ideas as we set about shaping the infant ACC.

What is the ACC and what does it do?

Aims and objectives

The objectives of the ACC are:

1. To become a recognised accrediting body for Christian counsellors, whether working within a pastoral setting, the wider community, or both.
2. To encourage high standards of training in Christian counselling.
3. To act as a resource for Christian counselling organisations.
4. To maintain a register of accredited counsellors and of appropriate organisations, including those which provide recognised Christian counselling training courses, caring homes and residential facilities.

Pastoral care undertaken within the authority structures of churches stands on its own and the ACC has no direct remit to monitor its quality. The association's function comes into play where local churches and para-church organisations also offer counselling services to the wider community.

Even where Christian counsellors are working solely within churches, they may wish to draw on the resources of the ACC – for example to improve the service they offer, or where a church member has a friend or relation in a different part of the UK who needs support. The ACC is available to help co-ordinate and support training for churches working in both pastoral and community settings. It offers continuing support for Christians who work as counsellors. It keeps a register of counsellors, teachers, clinics, training programmes and residential facilities, and updates it every three months. This details the training and experience of each individual or organisation, and will exclude any who do not satisfy the minimum level appropriate. If complaints are received against any individual or organisation and these are upheld by the subsequent investigation, that entry will be removed from the register.

Basis of faith

The ACC's simple statement of faith, to which all its members must accede, says that it 'affirms the central truths of the Christian faith, as expressed in the Bible and in the historic creeds. In particular, it affirms God as Triune, Father, Son and Holy Spirit, and is committed to expressing the lordship of Christ and the authority of Scripture in all areas of belief and practice.'

Christian carers and counsellors are encouraged to see their work in the context of Christ's manifesto to bring deliverance to *all* in need:

> To bring good news to the afflicted;
> He has sent me to bind up the brokenhearted,
> To proclaim liberty to captives,
> And freedom to prisoners;
> To proclaim the favorable year of the Lord
>
> (Isaiah 61:1–2, ASV).

The ACC believes that Christian counsellors can reach out to hurting people across what might be seen as barriers in all areas of life, including those of race, religion, culture, class, sex, gender, age, health and education.

Individual Christians and organisations show a great variety of approaches to counselling. Some are more comfortable than others in drawing on insights from secular theory and practice. While acknowledging this, the ACC seeks to act as a co-ordinating and monitoring body by recognising those Christian counselling services and training programmes which meet its high standards. As the ACC grows, more Christian counselling agencies are affiliating to it (as of January 1995 there were seventy-eight). It is hoped that the central organisation will have some role in spotting those who 'do the rounds' of endless counsellors without really being prepared to change and grow. They could then be offered appropriate help, but prevented from wasting large amounts of skilled people's time.

The main way in which the ACC seeks to encourage responsibility and accountability in all Christians who counsel is to offer an accrediting process which is widely acceptable to Christian churches and counselling organisations. It also facilitates discussion and negotiation on agreed standards of competence in counselling by Christians and seeks to negotiate with other institutions, such as Social Services, health authorities, chaplaincies, the British Association for Counselling and the Association for Pastoral Care and Counselling.

It is particularly important that counselling by Christians in the community should be comparable, in terms of competence and accountability, to that of colleagues trained in secular methods. As well as complying with the appropriate codes of ethical behaviour required of other counsellors, the ACC would expect the accredited Christian counsellor to work within Christian moral values under the lordship of Christ. Far from lagging behind in standards, training and accountability, the ACC aims to be a pace-setter for excellence.

The organisation and structure of the ACC

Briefly, the ACC is a charitable trust company overseen and controlled by its council. This meets once a year and all Christian counselling centres and training organisations which are accepted as participating members can appoint representatives to it. As well as acting as final authority in all matters, the council appoints the board to oversee the day-to-day running of the association and also the directors who are responsible for its charitable and legal functions. The board then appoints members of the accreditation and training committees.

Accreditation

The ACC's standards are known to be high and many statutory and voluntary bodies have appointed counsellors on the basis of their ACC accreditation. Normally people become trainee members of the ACC first. This does not indicate any degree of competence. It simply enables the accreditation committee to offer advice in helping the candidate choose further courses and practical experience so that he or she can complete the requirements for accreditation.

The ACC awards accreditation at three levels and in two settings: pastoral and community. It rarely expects anyone to apply for accreditation in both settings at the same time. Most members first apply for General Accredited membership in one or other setting. This indicates a general training and level of experience in Christian counselling. Those who have been accredited in one setting and later want accreditation in the other would have to undertake further courses and practical experience as appropriate, but not as much as if they were starting from scratch.

General Accredited members must complete a total of 250 hours of theoretical and practical counselling training in a recognised Christian counselling centre or training institute. Alternatively, they must undertake at least 100 hours on a Christian course or in a counselling centre recognised by the ACC. Of those 100 hours, half must be spent on a basic Christian counselling course. Some of the remaining 150 hours may be spent in secular-based training and practice. Applicants also submit two completed case histories taken from their previous year's practice. They supply a reference from a Christian leader who knows them well and can attest to their continuing growth in Christian maturity. Their supervisor gives another reference detailing the recent counselling experience and the competency of the applicant. Candidates have to show that they are keeping records of all counselling experience and agree to undertake further training in Christian counselling of at least twenty hours during the five-year validity period of their accreditation certificate.

Advanced Accredited members need an additional 350 hours of training or experience, making a total of 600 hours. At least 250 of those hours should have been spent on training in both the theory and skills of counselling, part preferably with an ACC-recognised Christian counselling course. The remaining 350 hours would consist of properly supervised counselling experience. This time three case histories, as well as the references, need to be submitted. An additional fifty hours of counselling training must be taken during the five-year validity of the Advanced Accredited certificate.

The third level is that of Supervisor Accredited membership. Normally applicants will already be accredited to the advanced level and they will have to provide a log, giving evidence of their counselling and supervisory experience over the past two years. They may provide references from counsellors they have supervised or from the director of the agency they work with. They also need references from another supervisor with whom they have discussed their counselling experience and competence as a supervisor.

The BAC requires more hours of training and experience than the ACC for its basic level of accreditation. In practice, only full-time counsellors can gain it. The ACC acknowledges that not everyone will be able to give all their time to counselling and this is why it has adopted a more stepped approach. Its highest levels of accreditation require more training and experience than the BAC does.

In addition, the ACC is looking into a level of accreditation for those involved purely within a small church or house-group setting. While less formal, this would still be structured. With its own training programme and monitoring procedure, it would provide a supportive system to meet a real need and to raise standards, without placing unrealistic time demands on small groups of people.

Supervision

Supervision enables counsellors to increase and improve their skills and to develop understanding and sensitivity to their own responses and feelings. It helps them to go further in understanding clients' feelings and to develop their own knowledge of God, of spirituality, of counselling theory, skills and processes and how these things relate together. Those counsellors who disregard the need for supervision run the risk of becoming stale, of missing important issues about themselves and their clients, or even, albeit unconsciously, of abusing their clients.

A counsellor's supervisor should not be a friend or immediate colleague, or collusion becomes a possibility. The counsellor needs to discuss his or her workload with an objective, experienced and qualified person working in a similar field. A supervisor is there to support and encourage, to help integrate godly theoretical knowledge and practice and to check that Christian and professional ethics, values and standards are maintained. However, just as it is vital that a client must not give responsibility for the issues in his life to his counsellor, the counsellor must not transfer responsibility, either for clients or himself, to his supervisor.

Supervision should not be regarded primarily as a time for advice-giving as in a teacher/pupil relationship. It will be a consultative process – thus the supervisor does not necessarily have to work with the same approach as the counsellor. The good supervisor creates an atmosphere where a counsellor's feelings can be readily and uncritically acknowledged and where case material can be explored within a confidential setting of contracts and boundaries.

Supervision should take place at least once a month, with sessions fixed in advance, not left until needed or convenient. Ideally both counsellor and supervisor will be covered by insurance and the supervisor will also have supervision.

Training

As I am the ACC's chairman of training, the training office is based at Barnabas Christian Resource Centre. I am currently writing up counselling training standards which will be implemented over the next five years. The ACC does not itself provide training courses, but validates the courses given by other organisations, provided they meet all the standards laid down.

The training committee is a panel of trainers, examiners and assessors. Its members come from all parts of the United Kingdom and are working in the field of counselling and training in church settings, community settings or in the academic world. They meet once a month to assess material sent in from training agencies, to look at standards and to offer ACC recognition to those who have successfully attained them.

The ACC recognises training both within the church (the pastoral setting) and in the community (the professional setting). It recognises training at the following levels:

1. Basic Introductory
2. Intermediate
3. Advanced
4. Specialist
5. Supervisory [1.2.3.]
6. Training the trainers [1.2.3.]

All of these courses can be run in the church setting or the community setting. The training committee works continually on a quality control programme. A certificate is issued to each training body for a period of five years and each organisation is given an individual registration number.

Ethics and code of practice

Counsellees are vulnerable and it would be easy to exploit them. The ACC points out that they should be kept fully informed and given the opportunity for discussion at every stage. Their integrity and safety should be maintained and all reasonable steps should be taken to seek appropriate medical or legal assistance. Before counselling begins, the basis of the relationship between counsellor and counsellee should be made explicit, preferably in writing, as should the policy on maintenance of records and limits of confidentiality. All Christian counsellors should receive pastoral care from the local church community, as well as appropriate supervision of their counselling.

The ACC lays down a thirteen-point code of practice which expands on its ethical basis as given above – for example, the counsellor should take all reasonable steps to ensure that the counsellee suffers neither physical nor psychological harm during counselling. Counsellors are responsible for working in ways which promote the counsellee's control over his own life. They should respect his ability to make decisions and to change in the light of his own beliefs and values.

Among other things, the code also looks at if, and under what circumstances, the counsellor should act on behalf of his client. It suggests that counsellors should preferably work in pairs but that a trainee counsellor should be present only if the client agrees.

Several points deal with the important matter of confidentiality. Normally records will be kept and the counsellee should know this, have access to them and be told the degree of security in which they are stored. The current law on computer data protection must be understood and observed. Confidentiality should never be breached in the context of prayer support, and the counsellor should gain his client's permission before conferring with other professional workers. If the counsellor feels that the client may cause serious physical harm to himself or others he may, after consultation with a supervisor or experienced counsellor, break confidentiality. Counsellors differ over whether they should do this if the client expresses a plausible intent to commit suicide.

Contracts

The ACC expects a written contract with the counsellee to be set up before counselling starts, and that all pre-counselling information should be full and accurate. The counsellee should also be given a written copy of the complaints procedure and how to further any complaint with the ACC, which has its own detailed complaints policy. Further details, and sample contracts, can be found in my book *Counselling in the Community* (see p. 252).

Professionalism

Again the ACC makes explicit its standards – that counsellors should be supervised and trained. They should work within their limits and be prepared to refer counsellees on where necessary. They should be prepared to explore and resolve conflicts of interest. They should not counsel if their functioning is impaired for any reason, such as personal or emotional difficulties, illness or alcohol. They should be accountable for all their dealings, including financial ones, and never act so as to bring counselling into disrepute. They must keep up to date in their understanding of laws which may affect their work and should seek legal advice where necessary.

They should keep a log-book of all counselling. Counsellors should take out a professional indemnity insurance where appropriate – usually insurance companies require accredited membership of an organisation such as the ACC before they will issue this and the ACC has a special arrangement for its members with one such company.

Opposition from the secular world towards Christian counsellors and the ACC

The secular world is often suspicious of Christian counsellors, especially those who work from a biblical base. There is a feeling that they have little or nothing to offer, or maybe that they will foist their beliefs on all and sundry. Whether working in the professions or solely within church settings, Christians in counselling need to challenge some of that thinking, as well as giving no ground for accusations of sloppy practice.

Every counsellor, of any religion or none, holds a worldview of some kind. In our pluralistic society counsellors are free to counsel those who do not share the same beliefs, provided that they work to professional standards and within an acceptable code of ethics. Of course the counsellor must be acceptable to the client and the autonomy of the client must be respected by the counsellor. The ACC works hard to ensure that these things happen.

Nevertheless, while setting up the ACC and working as a Christian in counselling, on occasions I have experienced conflicts with secular counselling organisations or individuals. Some people can be quite aggressive. For example, in 1994 I was travelling on a ship when a couple of Americans in the coffee queue started chatting to me and the man asked what job I did.

When I told them, the woman smiled with delight. 'Hey, I work as a counsellor too!'

As her husband turned away with a bored expression, she started questioning me enthusiastically. 'Tell me, what sort of counselling are you involved with?'

'Well, I'm a Christian and much of my work is done through churches.'

The woman glared at me for a moment, then turned her back and walked off.

I wasn't having that. 'Also, I use Rogerian and Egan models of counselling,' I shouted after her, knowing that most secular counsellors accept those gurus.

At that she came back and we sat down with our coffees to talk – which was fine so long as I kept to my experiences in social work. She could not tolerate any mention of the Christian side of my counselling practice.

When she had gone, a man who had been sitting at a nearby table lent over and tapped me on the shoulder. 'You'll forgive me for listening to your conversation,' he said with a smile. 'It's a boring journey and I'm intrigued. Tell me, how come a counsellor can be so aggressive? I thought ''non-directive'' was the key word – not telling others what to think!'

'That's true. You obviously know something about it.'

'A little – I'm a doctor. I find it strange that you've had more training and experience than that American, yet she wouldn't accept what you do because your value base is different from her own.'

The ACC provides a base from which Christian counsellors can challenge the assumptions of the many professionals who think like the woman on that ship – that only secular models of counselling work. Within the ACC, a Christian counsellor can receive all he needs, including the best standards of accreditation and training, while retaining his value base, thus being able to continue his counselling work.

Opposition from Christians

A secular psychiatrist once commented to me that the evangelical church is good at saving sinners but hopeless at rescuing its own, and he couldn't understand why. He had observed that a man with some deep problem or sin might come to a church, give his heart to God and be welcomed with open arms. On the other hand, someone already within the church who admitted to the same thing would be thrown out! It's as though Jesus, walking on the water and seeing Peter start to sink, had said, 'O you of little faith!' and shoved him under with his foot! Instead the Bible says, 'Immediately Jesus reached out his hand and caught him' (Matthew 14:31).

The psychiatrist went on to tell me that Christian clients of his had repressed their feelings for years, becoming weighed down by guilt. He said that he welcomed the birth of the ACC because it would set up safe opportunities for Christians to share their feelings. 'I have good training and experience, but as a non-believer I recognise that I'm not equipped to help these Christian people in certain areas,' he said.

If he understood, why do some Christians leave their heads behind when going to church? I really do wonder about church leaders I have met who seem unwilling to use the skills of professionals, even from within their own congregations. They can see no use for psychologists and ask, 'Why do we need trained counsellors? Hasn't God already equipped us to do all things?'

One member of my counselling team remarked, 'There are no problems in my church.' Into the surprised silence which followed she explained, 'We don't talk to each other for long enough to find out about them!'

Many churches are so activity orientated that they do not want to make time for people to work through painful issues in their lives. Counselling is viewed with suspicion because it can throw up such difficult problems and dilemmas, often appearing at first to make things worse for individuals and their families. So instead of being looked at, problems get pushed under the suface.

Some think that becoming a Christian is enough and so put their all into making new converts. They see counselling as a waste of time and believe that all sins and problems are dealt with the moment a person gives his life to Jesus. Surely, though, anyone who keeps half an eye open knows long-standing Christians who have deep emotional problems, ranging from nervous breakdowns and depression to feelings of ambivalence about gender. Many of us know those whose hurt has been deepened in church settings by a lack of real compassion or unskilled attempts to help. Is this really what Jesus meant to happen? These churches have not brought very good news to these people, and few there will travel far in being transformed into the likeness of Christ.

It is important that mind-sets change, for where Christian leaders perceive the ACC with its talk of accountability and setting standards as a threat, the reputation of good Christian counsellors may get damaged. Christians

will not be allowed to practise in the wider community if
they do not conform to the law on accreditation.

Counselling, accrediting organisations and the law

I keep my eye on the position of counselling in law, but it
is still rather hazy. In September 1994 the government
asked the organisation Consultants at Work to look at
standards in counselling with regard to National Vocational Qualifications. As I write, no standards are laid
down other than those set by accrediting organisations
such as the BAC and ACC. It would cost millions to set
up an organisation to enforce full legislation on counselling in this country. I think it far more likely that the
government will rely on a voluntary code of practice
which would be monitored by the accrediting organisations.

European standards are also being set. European law
tends to be chaotic and it is by no means clear whether
Britain will accept any EC legislation which might be laid
down in future. In any case, at present Britain is leading
the way over counselling standards within Europe.

The British government has decided to look at counselling only within the community setting and has no plans to
work towards accreditation or legislation covering those
working solely within church settings. I doubt it ever will.
Even so, society would quite reasonably expect a good
standard of service to be offered. Of course, where Christians offer a service to the wider community – through
general counselling or day centres, for example, or those
for the homeless or for single mothers – these centres will
be expected to fall in with all standards and guidelines.

PART THREE
Problems in Counselling

8

What Is the Problem?

Is therapy itself a problem?

I see many dangers ahead for counsellors in both pastoral and community settings. Over the past twenty-five years, the professional British counselling scene has been following the USA in putting pressure on counsellors and trainees to be in continual therapy themselves. I find this odd, because we do not demand that those learning to be dentists have all their teeth out, or that trainee social workers should have undergone sexual abuse.

If, as sometimes happens, the therapist transfers some of his or her own difficulties onto trainees, they may end up being damaged personally where they were fine before. Also, making all counsellors and students have professional therapy may encourage them to think in a warped fashion about the kinds of problems which really do need this sort of help. The danger is that they will see counselling as the only means of recovery, whereas I believe that it is only one of the methods which has a proven track record of helping people through their personal pain and difficulties.

Along with many other professionals, I believe that the professional counselling scene in the United Kingdom is creating a kind of merry-go-round which is in danger of not serving those clients who really are in need. Instead, one counsellor sees another counsellor, who sees a supervisor, who sees another supervisor, who sees a therapist. Of course it is true that on occasions counsellors may require counselling or support, and I firmly believe it is essential for all of them to have regular and highly skilled supervision.

There are great dangers, though, when people feed off each other – for example when a counsellor needs his client as much as or more than the client needs him. This is known as co-dependency and it has become a real issue. The USA has a co-dependency culture fed largely by the insurance system. Without its money, much counselling and other therapy would grind to a halt, which in my opinion would be a very good thing. Not only are people being ripped off, but an adolescent culture is created, where individuals no longer feel responsible for themselves.

Even in the UK I am surprised at how many of those who are accredited at the highest level within the Christian and secular fields become lost in the maze of co-dependency. Though highly skilled counsellors, they are feeding their own needs and unable to step off the merry-go-round. There is often no real expectation that clients will recover – therapists appear to believe that they will always need counselling.

Over the past twenty-five years I have seen large numbers of people with serious personal pain and problems of one kind or another. Whether Christians or not, none of them has needed perpetual counselling, and I would expect over 85% of my clients to recover within a six-to-twelve-month period. Those with a strong faith or positive value base may do so more quickly than the average person from the wider community, but others will get better as a result of family support, altered circumstances or a new environment – plus the counselling support they receive.

If counselling really needs to continue indefinitely, can it be said to have solved anything, or to work at all? Surely the only way to measure its value is by a continual assessment process. For agencies, I believe that this should come from an outside body, while individual practitioners might consider an audit of each individual case by a professional person working within the people business but outside of the counselling arena.

Though some professionals see formal counselling as a solution for everything and everybody, I believe that most people never need it at all. Some who receive it would doubtless have got better without its help. To take a medical analogy, consider a man who visits his doctor because he feels ill, and he is told that he has flu which will go away after a few days' rest. The man will probably feel better simply because his problem is diagnosed and he is reassured that nothing else is wrong. Daily visits to the doctor will not help him. Some patients, though, come with more serious conditions which really do need regular treatment from their GP or even a hospital specialist.

Is the church a problem or an asset?

There is no doubt that counselling has been of tremendous value to many people who need specialist help. It will continue to be so, but my experience tells me that the strongest of all supports is the individual's own value base. If the person is a Christian we need to build on this, not try to take it away or encourage him to look for alternatives. Circumstances can cause a person's faith to be shaken or even lost for a short period of time, but the loving care of God will pick him up again and bring him closer to God.

I firmly believe that the greatest therapy a Christian can have comes from his personal relationship with Jesus Christ and the Holy Spirit's working in his life. His faith gives him the opportunity to stand back from himself and hand over to the Lord all the difficulties, pressures and stresses which he feels. I have observed over and over again how a mixture of counselling and prayer ministry can speed recovery, and I feel that this is an area which merits more research.

As I said in Chapter 5, I find that problems in the pastoral and secular communities are often identical. However, when it comes to helping people and providing a healing environment, the church should be a tremendous asset. Open, loving, accepting groups of people can often help prevent serious damage from developing and help heal deep emotional wounds. Care and prayer, nurture and encouragement, hope and a new start – churches can give all these and more.

Also there is an enormous pool of skills within churches in areas such as parenting, counselling and teaching. These skills can be harnessed. Churches and other Christian organisations have set up some excellent schemes offering either general counselling into the community – such as Network in Bristol, Cardiff Concern or Manor House in Northampton – or specialist services such as that for single mothers in Stourbridge. Many more groups seek support and training, and I find this most encouraging. The quality of service offered is going up all the time.

Setting the scene for counselling

Before embarking on the next four chapters, which deal with some of the problems commonly found in counselling, I would like to say a little about beginning the counselling process. This is a very brief section on a huge and important subject, and a great deal has been written about it. Some helpful books are listed in the Appendix to this book.

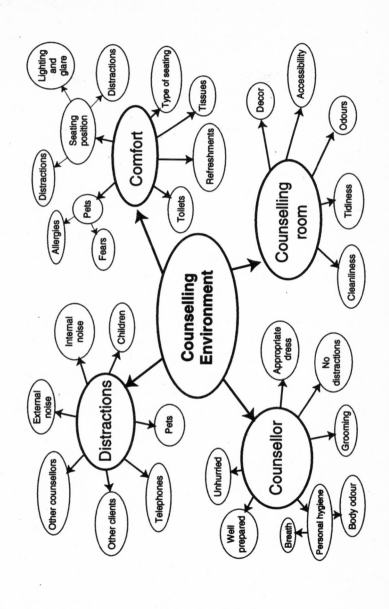

First of all there is the important matter of the physical environment. The room to be used for counselling needs to be comfortable and safe, with as few distractions as possible. (See diagram.)

The same applies to the counsellor or counsellors who take the session. Some counselling agencies insist that counsellors should be the same gender as their client; others do not. It is important to be aware of the dangers of over-involvement which cross-gender counselling can bring, especially in the more informal church settings where relationships are not confined to the formal counselling situation. The supervisor should help the counsellor look at this honestly and spot any problems which might develop.

In the initial interview the counsellor will be starting to build a relationship of trust with the client and also to set boundaries. He will 'presume nothing – check all things' and will give the client time in which to explore his history, his present situation and any worries about the future. (See diagram opposite.)

In that interview I will try to find out what the client needs and what he expects from counselling – the reasons why he has come. I will ask whether he has already received any help (from another counsellor, for example) or has done anything else towards solving his problems. I will ask about his medical background and whether he goes to a church. If not, I would make it clear that I work for a Christian organisation, but that although my faith affects the way I am as a person, I will not be trying to convert him or to talk about God at all, unless he requests that I do so. If he is a Christian, I will ask if his church supports him in coming for counselling or whether he is receiving any other pastoral help. I will also clarify whether prayer, Scripture reading and ministry would be acceptable to him within the context of counselling.

In terms of setting boundaries, I will read through our

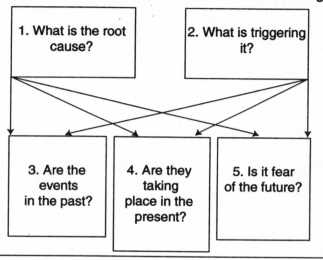

A counsellor must find the answers to the following:

If the counsellor does not clearly define the events that are taking place he will be unable to help the client, and the client and the counsellor could become frustrated and abort the counselling.

1. What is the root cause?

2. What is triggering it?

3. Are the events in the past?

4. Are they taking place in the present?

5. Is it fear of the future?

contract with the client and we will both sign it. This sets out our code of conduct, emphasising the autonomy of the client's own rights and choices, and the fact that he will be respected and not judged. The contract defines the limits of the vital matter of confidentiality over such issues as disclosures of dangerous or criminal activity, counsellor's supervision and note-taking. It explains our appointment system, complaints procedure, money matters and that the client remains responsible for his own actions. It also states that either side is free to terminate the contract at any time.

By the end of the first interview I would hope to have established what help the client and myself feel that he needs and have worked out whether I, or someone on my team, can help this particular person. If so we will formulate an ongoing plan which will include how often we see the client. If not I will try to refer him to another person or agency who can help.

The problem of pain

I am sometimes asked whether counselling can do more harm than good in getting people to explore painful areas in their lives. Certainly many will appear to get worse before they become better. People can become adept at denying pain by simply pretending that it is not there. For example, many with toothache will perform all kinds of mental gymnastics to avoid visiting the dentist, because they fear that he may cause them further discomfort before making them better.

A couple of trips to the dentist usually sorts everything out, whereas counselling can take months. How do people cope with the pain while carrying on with their everyday lives? Many still have to work and care for children and other family members. The counsellor should try to help clients find some strategy, or their pain will spill out in all the wrong places. Some may become angry or tearful with those close to them; a few may turn destructiveness towards themselves. Others may back-track and repress their pain until it emerges in the form of an illness, stress or depression.

A counsellor needs to think carefully before embarking on a series of sessions with a client who is likely to have reservoirs of suppressed pain. Is this a good time in his life to deal with it or would circumstances suggest that it would be best left for a while? Does the client have a support network at home to help him?

Once counselling has started the client may begin show-ing signs of distress when certain subjects are touched upon. He may say something like, 'My head's done in,' or, 'I've gone to pieces.' It is important to stop and acknowledge this – to say, 'It's OK to cry, or shout, or whatever – we'll go with this now.' The counsellor can then ask the client to explore what has triggered his response. It might not be words; it could be anything from a certain smell to the clothes one of you happens to be wearing. The counsellor can encourage the client to see something positive in the experience, for he will have found a key which will open the door to his feelings.

His pain is part of his life and history. If he can learn to acknowledge and confront it, without letting it dominate him, then he will develop his character. He needs to do this in a safe and appropriate place, such as a counselling session. There he can let go and respond in a full, child-like way, which might not be helpful in other circum-stances. When he leaves the session he can place the deeply hurting part of himself in a safe place behind the 'door' again, but this time he knows how to unlock it whenever he needs to examine the pain again.

Should acute pain surface between counselling sessions the counsellor can ask him to write down his feelings and what triggered them, so that both can explore them together in the next session. The important thing is that the client learns to be in control of his pain rather than having it dominate his life.

Aim of the following chapters about problems

I have noticed that despite their strong interest in helping people, many trainee counsellors have little idea of what goes on in our society. Most are profoundly shocked at case histories which, by the scale of what can happen, professionals would consider mild. On my courses I only use case studies which are well documented – in the courts, for example – yet many of my students find it hard to believe that some of these things can take place. Sometimes I wonder what the average pastor or person in the pew would think.

Christians often shy away from real pain on their doorsteps. They would rather hold a celebration meeting or plan to evangelise India – from a distance! Some pack off hurting church members to a doctor, which is at least better than launching into untrained, bungling attempts to help. The problems which counsellors deal with are deeper than they were a few years ago, and those who do not go into this field with their eyes open are in danger of causing further damage.

We need to know at least the obvious pitfalls, and what not to do. There is no room for naivety. Christians should assist those who want to equip themselves to help, by making sure they have the means to adopt the proper standards, training and practice.

The next four chapters are illustrated by true, if disguised, stories of what goes on in the real world. Unfortunately there is only space to deal in a surface manner with some of the points I feel are important about the more common problems we come across.

9

Family Issues

Marriage difficulties

Marriage can be one of the most complicated areas to counsel, especially if one partner wants help and the other does not. The church could do a good deal before conflicts happen, by setting up forums where young people can discuss the issues prior to marriage, and afterwards. We can all help by encouraging honest communication. Of course no one wants people intruding, but every marriage has hiccups from time to time and we all need to be able to talk to someone about them without feeling condemned.

Further down the line, where people realise they have serious problems and come for counselling, often we find that the root cause of the breakdown of their marriage is not adultery but the fact that the partners have nothing in common. We see many middle-class, respectable, intelligent people who throw themselves into all sorts of worthy activities. Years previously, however, they stopped communicating with each other or choosing to spend any time together, and so started growing apart. Now too hurt to face sharing their pain with each other or with friends, the couple acknowledge that their relationship is at an end. When the children go to university or leave home permanently, their parents' marriage either blows up or simply falls apart.

I have heard many wives say, 'I knew when I was walking up the aisle that he was the wrong man for me!'

'What did you feel when you first met him?' I ask. *My* mum said she knew when I had fallen in love because I started washing myself and asking for clean socks! But this woman might tell me that the young man she married had been an enthusiastic youth leader in her church, while she was a talented musician. Because they worked well together, a self-appointed church matchmaker had decided that they should wed. The whole church can exert quite a pressure to marry rather than remain single. After all, there's a lot of temptation in the world. Also the Bible says, 'Do not be yoked together with unbelievers' (2 Corinthians 6:14). The difficulty arises if certain people conclude that the few single people in a local church must all be destined to marry among each other.

In our 'typical' case the matchmaker invited the young man and woman round for a meal – no hidden agendas, of course! In conversation, she dropped the suggestion quite casually that they would make a lovely couple. They both respected this older married lady, and wondered if perhaps she might be right – and so their relationship began. But they woke up to discover that he had married a musician and she a youth leader. They did not really know each other as people at all.

Such couples can exist in a loveless marriage for twenty or thirty years. A counsellor's only hope is to try to work on any areas which they might have in common. I attempt to find out if there is anything they like about each other. It is also important that both are clear about whether they really want the marriage to work. If not, the counsellor can do little, for the marriage was to all intents and purposes over before the couple ever came for counselling.

We saw a Christian couple who had functioned quite well as a family while the wife stayed at home caring for their three children. By the time these had become a little more independent, 'Anne' was in her mid-thirties. She had trained in design before her marriage and her considerable skills in that area stood her in good stead when she started working for the multi-national company of which her husband was a director. Soon she was promoted and started travelling the world on company business. She gained confidence by the day, and came to realise that there was more to life than church and family. Her work took her away from home to hotels and restaurants, where she drifted into a relationship with another man who worked for the company.

After twelve months her husband found out. She broke off the adulterous relationship and wanted to repent before God, but Anne was not sure if she wanted her marriage to continue, for she felt that she had overtaken her husband in many ways. He yearned for reconciliation and for everything to return to how it was, but failed to see that his wife had changed and that they would have to work at finding some common ground. They lived in separate bedrooms in the same house while we attempted to counsel them and their children.

Statistics show that for the last five years women have brought more divorce proceedings than men have. This is reflected in the church, especially with women in their forties or fifties. Many, like Anne, who start work again or go to college, begin to see that their potential is greater than they had realised. This can create problems for the husband, as it takes a big man to accommodate change and growth in a wife who perhaps always used to run around after him and think him wonderful.

Marriages also break down where the man feels the need to dominate, manipulate and control his wife. Some do this because they are insecure, or because they follow role models set by their father or even by an admired church minister. Male domination can be especially prevalent among Christians where St Paul's teaching on wifely submission has been misquoted and misemphasised. Husbands believe they have *carte blanche* to behave in a selfish and domineering way inside their homes, though most would never dream of behaving in that way to anyone outside of them.

Many Christian women believe that it is sinful to complain or even to disagree with their husbands, until one day they come to the end of their tether and realise that their marriage will never work. At that point they feel guilty before God and come for counselling, but it is often too late. They are worn out and feel that enough is enough. A counsellor can help build up their self-esteem, but unless the husband is also willing to change, this may cause further problems in their home, and sometimes with their church as well.

Marriage is a huge subject and I cannot write about all the aspects here, but I will just mention that adversity can show up problems within a marriage which had appeared to be fine. A serious illness or the death of a family member, the pregnancy of a teenage daughter or the divorce of a grown-up son can highlight weaknesses. The couple may feel that they need the help of a counsellor to work through these.

Leaders' marriages

Church leaders whose marriages are in trouble often hide their pain and problems for years. Such people feel that they are not allowed to make mistakes; that they must remain whiter than white. Many denominations have discouraged their ministers from pursuing friendships within the church, fearing that this would show favouritism. So a pastor and his wife may have no one with whom they can be honest and open, sharing their weaknesses as well as their strengths. Because they are not truthful about their marriage, the whole problem assumes the huge proportions of a guilty secret. They feel both shame and isolation. Their sense of desperation grows, putting yet more strain on the marriage. Where the wife has a career of her own, the couple can grow poles apart, until they have nothing in common except the children, and often precious little time for them.

On the outside all can appear fine – they may even be held up as an example for all to follow. But though they may have been living in the same house for twenty years, they have been living a lie, and when the truth explodes out it can be devastating for the church.

Divorce

Statistics show 150,000 divorces a year in England and Wales – the highest rate in Europe. More than one in three marriages end this way. There used to be few divorces among evangelical Christians, but that is no longer true. More and more families are torn apart, including those of pastors, church leaders and youth leaders.

For some couples, their marriage has been so horrendous and violent that by the time they come for counselling, it is over. In others, communication has irretrievably broken down and any love which they might once have felt for each other has ended. One or both partners may still have a deep faith in God and continue to attend church. Their desire to divorce may cause conflict for both church and counsellor.

What is the Christian response if, after many weeks of counselling in which we have explored every avenue, the couple still decide to go for a legal separation or divorce? We know from Scripture that divorce is not the perfect will of God. Some Christian organisations refuse to stand by a couple who have made up their minds to go through a divorce, but I would have to be critical of marriage and advice groups which take that attitude.

Whether a situation is referred to me by a solicitor or church, or by the couple themselves, I would not like to retreat to some high moral ground and turn them away. That would only leave them feeling angry, let down and confused.

While not necessarily condoning what is happening, I do recognise that people need unconditional love and support during what is likely to be one of the most painful periods of their lives. It may take a couple of years before all the people involved resettle and begin to find their way forward out of a state of complete brokenness. I cannot abandon them in their pain at this time, especially if children are involved. Even if the children have grown up and left home, many will need to cry and cry, and the counsellor must not forget them.

I feel that the role of the Christian counsellor and of the church is to care for people and to rescue our own – even when we dislike or disagree with the things they do. If the church deserts those who have gone through divorce they will tend to join other groups. That is one reason why I am pleased that more churches are beginning to show compassionate rather than judgemental attitudes to divorcees.

Violence within marriage

In the last five years I have been surprised by the number of women who have asked for counselling at Barnabas House because they could no longer tolerate continual violence from their husbands. I do not believe that the incidence of wife-beating has increased. It is simply that women in today's climate are no longer prepared to suffer in silence, and quite rightly so. At last battered wives are beginning to find the courage to say, 'I am not prepared to go home unless he changes, or something is done!'

But it is not easy for them. Realistically, the marriage can never work unless the man admits to the issues that are going on in his life and takes responsibility for his actions. Some even refuse to concede that any violence has taken place!

On one occasion a doctor and I were helping a lady called 'Wendy', who had acute depression. As the counselling session progressed it became obvious that she was suffering from some kind of physical pain.

'Are you feeling OK?' the doctor asked.

'No – my back is hurting me.'

The doctor asked me to leave the room while she examined her patient and then, after a short period, called me to the door again. As she lifted the back of Wendy's sweat-shirt I could see a mass of new wounds and old scars. The reason for her depression became clear. Her clergyman husband had subjected her to immense physical and emotional pressure for nearly the whole of her married life, yet he ran a respected Christian church in a middle-class area of that town.

Wendy told us that she did not want anything to come out into the open for fear that her husband would lose his position as minister and thus the family's livelihood and home. She also admitted to being terrified of what her husband would do to her if the doctor or myself attempted to talk to him about his violence. It is hard to know what to do in a position like this. My organisation has a strict code of ethics concerning confidentiality – as does the medical profession – but both the doctor and myself could see that Wendy risked serious injury or even death at the hands of her husband.

After many weeks of counselling Wendy agreed with us that the best course of action was for her to come away from the marital home for a period of time. This gave us the opportunity to work with her husband. At first, livid that his wife had told us what was going on, he responded to us with aggression. But soon he realised that he needed help, for he did not want to lose his wife. She too desired reconciliation, provided that he brought an end to the physical and emotional abuse.

The minister told us about his family background. His mother had suffered violence at home. To him it seemed the norm. I thought back to my time in the assessment centre, when adolescent boys would hit female members of staff, but never male ones. They were simply following behaviour patterns which they had learned from fathers, uncles or big brothers at home. We spent many months exploring the issues, looking at the minister's behaviour patterns and also having discussions together with Wendy so that we could identify any underlying causes or triggers of the aggression in his relationship with her.

All this time they were living apart, to the disgust of their church which felt that God had called them together and that Wendy had no business running off, no matter what had happened. We found ourselves in conflict with the church, because we believed that the couple's temporary separation would not necessarily lead to divorce and disaster. In fact we saw it as the only safe way forward. We did work through the deep hurts of both Wendy and her husband, despite the complex situation, and eventually saw reconciliation and healing start to take place. Today Wendy lives in the family home with her husband and no longer suffers abuse.

I firmly believe that where serious physical harm has been perpetrated over a number of years, it will be necessary to remove either the husband or the wife from the home. Then both can seek help. I would give clients a list of appropriate safe places, or suggest someone they could contact to help them find such a place – though some secular counsellors would think this was being too directive.

If a battered wife plucks up courage to bring matters to a head and a temporary or permanent separation results, she will experience overwhelming feelings of hurt, bitterness, anger, loss and even guilt. She needs a high level of support and especially the space to express her feelings in a safe environment. Because she will fear being in a situation where a man is in control, it is essential at this point that her counsellor is female. I would always work with a female lead-counsellor in this situation.

I am writing about this subject at more length than many because I have been shocked at the sheer number of women who have told me of how their husbands have beaten them – maybe over periods of ten to fifteen years. We have referrals every week of serious cases which come via solicitors, churches or the women themselves. Unfortunately, a number of these have, like Wendy, been wives of church ministers. When I talk about domestic violence on counselling courses, it is not uncommon for two or three women to come forward and say, 'This is happening to me.' The emotional damage in each case is hard to imagine and it will take a skilled counsellor a good deal of time before these women begin to find help. Yet society as a whole, and the church in particular, is often reluctant to admit that violence exists within marriage, especially in 'respectable' homes. Perhaps I should just mention here that there are other sorts of violence in the home – husband- or granny-battering, for example – but I have seen relatively few cases of these. The physical abuse of children is usually dealt with by Social Services.

But why do some Christian men beat their wives? Church-goers are often wrongly taught that emotions are unimportant or sinful, and so they suppress them. That is like trying to plug a volcano – the powerful feelings only surface later in some damaging way. Church leaders in particular may have no one with whom they can share their negative feelings. A few take out their aggression and anger on their wives or on other people weaker than themselves.

Men who are violent within the secrecy of their homes usually present a competent, outgoing facade, but on the inside they feel fearful and insecure. Emotionally, they are often stuck at the stage of adolescence or pre-adolescence. They seldom attack their children, often making good fathers until their offspring reach their teen-age years. When this happens the presence of two genera-tions of 'adolescents' in the same house often brings out conflicts. However, by then the daughter is able to look after herself or shout for help. Offspring don't seem to get locked into the situation in the same way as the wife does.

However, if children have seen their father showing physical, emotional or verbal aggression towards their mother over a number of years, a similar pattern of violence may well wreck their own marriages, even if they are Christians, and it would be wise to offer help before it comes to this.

Some other marital issues

Pre-marital counselling
Sex in marriage
Family planning
Problems with pregnancy
Infertility – raising questions of surrogacy and artificial
    insemination
Extra-marital sexual relationships and associated problems
    when these bring sexually transmitted diseases into
    marriage
Unresolved gender issues
Jealousy
Rebuilding the relationship after an enforced separation –
    eg where the husband has had to work abroad or spent
    time in prison
Remarriage
The single parent

Widows and widowers
The unmarried - singleness

Children and adolescents

'This youth is rotten from the bottom of their hearts; the young people are malicious and lazy; they will never be as youth happened to be before; our today's youth will not be able to maintain our culture.' These words were carved on a 3,000-year-old stone tablet in the ancient city of Babylon.

The generation gap hasn't changed much. One morning parents wake up to find that their nice conforming little daughter refuses to trot off to Brownies or Sunday school. She has turned into something called an adolescent. What that is no one knows, but it no longer communicates (except about saving the whale), wears clothing so strange that it only dares venture out after dark, reacts violently to the suggestion that it might benefit from a trip to that pit of deepest horror known as Marks and Spencer, and spends hours treating the bathroom to strange 'Shake and Vac' rituals with powders and lotions.

Glenys and I see adolescents migrate into a nearby art college every academic year, wearing dustbin liners and other strange plumage. We try to be kind to them. After all, each is the child of someone! However, we have found that adolescents may not respond well to a counsellor. In practice, many of us are middle aged and it can prove hard to find common ground on which to establish a helpful relationship. A generation gap most certainly does exist and youth culture is changing all the time. Obviously I saw a tremendous number of adolescents during my years in social work, but now my approach tends to be, 'Give them to someone who understands youth problems – a youth leader, for example. He applied for the job, he deserves them!'

To be more serious, I feel that young people of this generation have far more insight than we did in the 50s and 60s, and we can learn a great deal from them. But they do need someone to talk to about their hopes and fears, their conflicts, their feelings of helplessness and inability to cope and their problems in relating to others. Well-trained youth leaders are the ideal people, for they understand this generation's culture and the pressures they come under.

I find it sad that one of the major influences on young teenage girls today is a magazine called *Just 17*. Despite its name, it has a wide readership among thirteen-year-olds, who like to think of themselves as much older. These girls come in all shapes and sizes, but very few are going to match up to the ideal role models which this magazine presents when it comes to skin, hair, eyes, figure and hunkiness of boyfriend. Nor can they afford the ever-changing make-up, designer clothes and other trappings. Young girls are left feeling that they can never come up to standard. Some may wonder if there is something wrong with them. They then start reading the rest of the magazine which deals with teenage problems such as anorexia, drugs and alcohol.

The teens are a time for finding out about the world, and adolescents have always experimented, but if the media start presenting too much detail to those at the young end of the spectrum, is it surprising that some take on a copycat approach? A whole peer group of friends can talk and whisper and get drawn in. If it is seen as grown-up to experience anorexia, for example, some will be encouraged to follow that route.

In recent years we have seen a massive increase in teenage problems such as eating disorders and solvent abuse. More teenagers than ever run away from home and end up living on the streets. Of course we cannot blame all of this on the media. Many young people feel that no one is interested in hearing what they have to say. It is true that in many cases adults simply do not listen. Most have incredibly short memories of the time when they themselves were adolescents.

To make matters worse, churches and Christian books often teach about an unreal kind of model teenager. Far from scaling the heights of worldly sophistication, this one reaches moral perfection, with no faults, doubts or questions. He conforms in everything, obeying his elders and betters at all times. Church leaders, in particular, are expected to have their offspring well in control, or they don't deserve to be leaders – St Paul said so (1 Timothy 3:4–5).

Many teenagers in the church realise that they are being asked to conform to false standards. Those who want to know more of God for themselves often ask difficult questions such as, 'Why are things always done this way?' or, 'What's wrong with loud music?' They kick against being made to conform to traditional moulds. When they turn up at church with ripped jeans and one ear-ring, everyone stares. Back home, embarrassed parents read the riot act. But it is often the parents who need help to deal with their own anger rather than the adolescents who need counselling.

I say to them, 'He's only expressing himself like any normal, healthy person of his age. Aren't you pleased that he wants to go to church at all?'

One couple brought their teenage daughter, Megan, to see me. They felt that she had tremendous problems and put these down to the fact that they had adopted her.

Megan soon made it clear that she had no interest in talking to me, so I suggested that she joined my own young teenage daughter, who was watching *Neighbours* in another room.

'Oh no,' said her father in alarm, 'she's not allowed to watch TV! Certainly not programmes like *that*, anyway!'

Though surprised, I respected his wishes and asked my daughter if she would turn off the television and talk to Megan instead.

'You can swap stories about your terrible parents, if you like!' I said.

All that I had seen or heard about Megan suggested that she had no deep-seated problems stemming from rejection by her natural parents in early childhood. On the other hand I could see that this couple who loved her were suddenly experiencing something for which they were not prepared. Their first child had reached adolescence. That can be a tough time. Sometimes it's the parents and dog who long to run away from home, never mind the youngsters!

Later I found out that Megan did watch *Neighbours* and other programmes regularly – round the corner from home, at her friend's house. Forced into a corner, she felt that she had to live a lie. Her parents had forbidden something which all her classmates enjoyed and it had damaged her relationship with them.

I told them, 'Look, Megan's going to church, she has a desire for God, but she's living in a culture where teenagers are taught to express themselves. She's old enough to make up her own mind, to choose her own clothes and music and TV programmes – within reason. Remember, her tastes may be very different from yours. You need to be completely sure that you're not stopping her doing things simply because they embarrass you.'

Megan's parents were tremendous. They listened carefully and re-examined their own value base. They ensured that their relationship with Megan included less conflict and fewer straight 'no's'. They began to worry less and to appreciate the good in her. They had simply needed educating.

Very little help is normally given in the difficult business of bringing up teenage children. Even the most loving

parents do not automatically know how to do it. This is
one reason why we now run a training course in parenting.
It highlights the different stages which children go
through and stresses that all will not necessarily follow
a neat pattern, even in the most well-balanced family.

More help is generally available for parents of younger
children. Health visitors and others are quick to give
advice on how to deal with babies or the 'terrible twos'.
From the age of three to five, small children go through
what I call the 'me–now–no' syndrome: making demands,
wanting their own way and creating hell if they do not find
satisfaction immediately. I see the same thing emerging,
quite normally, in the early teenage years. If parents,
schoolteachers or others suppress this too vigorously, I
have noticed that it will often show up to ruin the early
years of marriage.

'We're going out to buy the paint *now*,' snaps one
partner. 'I don't care if you are in the middle of doing
something else, and it's tough if you don't like the colour.
If I can't have my dining room decorated in bright orange,
I'm pouring that sickly green gunge you bought all over
your stupid head!'

When I was in social work, a family came to see me.
Their son Jon had been put into the care of the Local
Authority as he was said to be 'beyond parental control'. He had been in trouble with the police for stealing
and had spent some time in prison. He had also made a
number of girls pregnant.

I looked at the three of them, sitting in my office on that
stifling August afternoon, twenty years ago. The young lad
had a Mohican hairstyle and tattoos all over him. The
message on his right hand read, 'Love, hate!' His father
sweltered in a three-piece suit, with every button done up
and his mother had all but disappeared under a grey coat
which reached to her ankles. She wore her hair scraped
back into a tight bun. They had forbidden Jon to play

football or to wear the same clothes as everyone else at
school and allowed him to associate only with those who
belonged to his narrow church denomination.

'I hate them!' intoned Jon, and despite all my experience of difficult teenagers, I had never seen such loathing
in anyone's eyes. 'I'll get my own back – just wait!'

I felt greatly concerned that Jon would inflict emotional,
if not physical, damage on his parents as revenge for his
strict background. Later I lost contact with the family.
Years passed before one day I saw Jon getting out of a
BMW car. He looked quite different and had with him a
young lady and a baby.

'Jon?' I called across the street. 'You seem to be doing
well!' I walked over to talk to him.

'Hey, it's Mr Altman! Have you met my wife Sheila and
my little baby?' he asked, with obvious pride.

'Well, this is quite a change!' I said, shaking hands.
'Would you object if I asked what happened?'

'Those were bad times,' he agreed, 'but I went to work
in a factory. Saw this girl in the office – even weirder than
me – her hair all over the place. Well, I fell for her. Didn't
realise she was the director's daughter, did I? He said that
if I wanted her I'd have to work my way up. So I did.
Went to college and everything. Few years back, we
married.' He put his arm round his wife. 'And no, Mr
Altman – we didn't have to!'

'Well, that's wonderful for both of you! But . . . would
you mind telling me . . . what happened to your parents?
What sort of relationship do you have with them now?'

Jon looked sad. 'I don't see them any more. Sheila's a
Roman Catholic, see? When I married her they said they
wanted nothing more to do with me. It cuts me up, because
look at their lovely grandchild! But they won't come
near.'

Jon's story showed me so clearly that if people put rigid
structures before relationships, they can destroy every-

thing. The real reason why many parents prevent their teenager from doing certain things is not to protect him from certain danger, but to save themselves embarrassment among their own peers. Perhaps the best advice is to love your child and give him enough rope, but keep hold of the end so he knows that if he needs help, you are there.

To be honest, I believe that young people have a great deal to offer. Most will not turn to drugs or suicide, become pregnant while still at school or create riots. Even those whose teenage years are stormy will nearly all go on to become responsible, mature adults who take their place in society. Those who go wrong do not all come from dreadful homes. It is possible for the most loving, well-adjusted, sensible and godly family to produce monsters. We are all individuals with free will and it is important that we do not condemn parents for the behaviour of their offspring, but rather offer them help and support.

Helping men who have not been fathered themselves

In recent years I have counselled a number of men who had little real relationship with their fathers. Some have come from privileged backgrounds and were either away at public school themselves or their fathers travelled a good deal on business. Many of these fathers gave their sons everything they wanted materially, but never developed a real relationship with them. Missionaries' children can suffer too when they are sent away to be educated in this country. In both cases the fathers may be successful in their own terms, but their children remember them as figures who shouted and disciplined, not as dads who played and chatted and took delight in them.

When these boys become grown men, they see their elderly fathers still as unapproachable, authoritarian figures. Many enjoyed a good relationship with their mothers, but somehow that is not enough, and because they lack a role model, many have no idea how to play with their own children. Sometimes in counselling I use play, keeping a box of Lego handy or putting some toys on the floor. It is refreshing to see men in their thirties – barristers, pastors or teachers – playing for the very first time. As they do so they often tell me about how isolated and angry they felt as children.

I have found that a man like this can be stuck in adolescence emotionally – afraid to make any decision for himself or his family without consulting his father. In this situation I would have to beware the danger of transference – many would like me to become the ideal father they long for. But obviously the counsellor's role is to help them develop into full adult people themselves.

Once I counselled a doctor called Matthew who wanted to work through certain things from his childhood. His father had shown more interest in the church and evangelism than he had in his young son. This had left Matthew with many negative feelings. After we had talked them through I encouraged him to give them over to God, but he struggled for months.

Finally he said, 'If I'm ever really going to let go of all this I need to do something tangible, something physical!'

I had no ideas, but the next week he turned up with a large kite which he had made out of white paper. On it he had written words like 'rejection', 'hurt', 'isolation' and 'insecurity'. He detailed all the areas where he felt he had been let down by his father, such as, 'Always told what to do; never asked for my opinion.' Then he went outside and ran round the common, trailing the paper kite.

A puff of wind caught it. 'I must let it go! I must let it go!' Matthew shouted, still holding tight. I saw how difficult this was for him, and for a moment wondered if he would ever release the string. Finally he unclenched his hand and watched as the kite soared off into the clouds.

His face relaxed. 'Now I know it's really gone. I can live for me. I'm free to love my wife and kids and to have real relationships at last.'

Some other family issues

1. Children and parents. Problems with parenting, including babies and bringing up young children. School and learning difficulties. Bullying.

Adoption – from the points of view of child and parents. Mothers whose children are adopted. Adults who were adopted as children and later sought their real parents – the effect of this on both families. Surrogacy. Fostering.

Unwanted pregnancy within marriage. Unwanted children, or parents who wanted a child of the other gender. Pre- and post-abortion counselling.

Children who have been in care, adapting to life in society, to marriage, etc.

2. The family. Normal and abnormal family dynamics (the counsellor may have to understand family life in different cultures and also different family types). Problem families. The family in crisis.

10

Adult Victims of Sexual Abuse and Gender Issues

Adult victims of sexual abuse

Over the past ten years an increasing number of people have come for counselling because they suffered sexual abuse as children, and this is causing them problems as adults. Glenys was amazed that during her first few weeks working for Barnabas House full time, every client she saw had suffered from sexual abuse during childhood. She had never come across this problem before – or not so as to be aware of it. She had no clear idea of who would come for counselling, half-expecting homeless people or those with marriage difficulties. She certainly did not seek out clients who had been abused, yet they came in large numbers.

Such survivors of abuse come from every walk of life, including professionals from respectable, well-off families. I have seen many who were severely abused within a church setting, and that would cover a wide spectrum of denominations, from evangelical and house churches to high Anglicans and Roman Catholics.

The church and the abuser

Initially, some quarters of the church responded with strong anger and denial whenever sexual abuse was mentioned, but statistics and a number of court cases have proved that it is far from uncommon in the Christian community. Some former church leaders, as well as other Christians, are serving long prison sentences for the sexual abuse of children.

Amazingly, churches can try to sweep known abuse under the carpet. Bishops have covered up situations and allowed them to continue. In recent years, the damage that abuse does has become more widely known, yet denominational leaders have chosen to ignore what was going on or taken the attitude that it was 'not too serious'. In other cases churches have split over whether a member who has been caught abusing children should be handed over to the law. It is important that churches – along with any organisations which care for children – are fully aware of the law and are fulfilling their responsibilities under it. Of course, once they do this a whole series of procedures will swing into operation. (See diagram on p. 168.)

It came to light recently that a total of eleven children from the same church, plus several who are now in their teens and early twenties, were all abused by their vicar over a period of years. I suspect that there are more who have not yet come forward. My organisation is involved in counselling many of the parents. The vicar is now in prison, yet the mothers had regarded him as a warm, lovable person.

'Lots of us women in the church used to cook his meals and do his washing – he was single, you see,' one told me. 'And when my son said he didn't want to go to Eurodisney with him, I gave him such a lecture about how kind the vicar was to raise the money and give his time to take a group of them all that way!' She shook her head. 'We mothers never listened to our children. We never suspected a thing!' A certain childish vulnerability about the vicar had won over the motherly hearts of the good ladies of this church, while all the time he was inflicting

SOCIAL SERVICES PROCEDURE
CHILD PROTECTION TEAMS

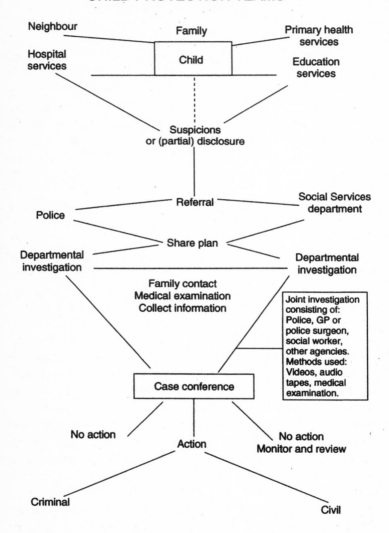

severe abuse and untold damage on their children. The fact is that an abuser knows where groups of children gather and will often find jobs in schools or social work – or gravitate to churches where he or she may win a child's trust through a Sunday school or young people's group.

To most human beings it seems almost inconceivable that anyone should want to hurt a child in this way, especially if that person claims to follow Jesus. Sometimes I am asked, 'Can an abuser be a Christian?' Perhaps only God can answer that question. I would not like to sit on the seat of judgement. One factor may be that, statistically, 40% of abused children go on to become abusers themselves. All I know for sure is that abusers should never be allowed to work with children.

Of course, adults within a church tend to trust one another, and we would not want it any other way. While staying aware, we have to be careful that fear of abuse does not kill love and make us all losers. Air crashes too are terrible things. I know that they can happen very occasionally, but that does not prevent me travelling by plane. Parents can become over-protective towards their children, never letting them spend the night at a friend's house, for example. It is important to keep a sense of proportion and to realise that most people are not abusers.

On a family skiing holiday, I watched the instructor catching my teenage daughter as she hurtled down the slopes. He was handling her in an entirely appropriate way. They were both laughing and thoroughly enjoying themselves. I felt sad that as a social worker I could never treat another person's child as he was doing. Teachers are told that they cannot hug a little one who has quarrelled with her friend or fallen over in the playground, yet children need physical comfort and affection. Sadly, abuse has changed things for all of us and the system designed to prevent its twistedness has robbed us all.

On the other hand, looking back, I am horrified by the way I behaved at youth camps. In my late teens myself, I used to pick up thirteen- or fourteen-year-old girls and hurl them into the sea. It was good clean fun and I had no sinister motivation, but some of those girls might well have been in the care of the Local Authority because they had suffered abuse. Hindsight tells me that I was not handling them in a helpful or appropriate way.

Abuse victims

Working in the observation and assessment centres, I was responsible for many children who had been abused. I had to help prepare court cases and thought I knew quite a bit about the subject. Even so, I have been surprised by the number of adult survivors of abuse who have come for private counselling. Current thinking says that depending on the precise definition of abuse (physical, emotional and sexual), between one in four and one in ten suffer from it at some point in their childhood. In other words, every one of us will know many victims and adult survivors.

Normally we do not counsel child victims at Barnabas House, as they come under the Social Services and are likely to be involved in court cases. The youngest 'adult' we have seen was seventeen and the oldest a lady of eighty-six. Most of these were systematically abused as children for many years within the church or wider community.

Over the past two or three years, the number of male survivors coming forward has increased dramatically. Many have been abused within public schools. Unfortunately, in some cases the perpetrator was a religious man, which can be particularly devastating.

After I spoke at a church service one day, a young lawyer came up to me. He told me that he had been severely abused by a chaplain at public school over a period of six years. It had left him feeling unsure about his identity, and when he met an attractive young female law student he had no idea how to handle his feelings. Was he falling in love? Was he homosexual or heterosexual? He had not experienced any kind of sexual relationship since he left that school at the age of fourteen.

I spent time talking to him. After a while he saw that the abuse had robbed him of his childhood, and eventually he realised that it was not his fault. We worked through many of the issues and later I was invited to his wedding. He and the former law student have continued to enjoy a stable marriage.

Not the root of all evil

Obviously sexual abuse, though much more common than was once thought, is not the cause of everyone's problems. The counsellor with a run of clients who have been abused must beware of reading hidden abuse into every situation. It is essential that counsellors at no time suggest or even hint to clients that they may have been abused as children, and I would certainly include 'words of knowledge' in this proscription (see Chapter 13).

A mother asked Glenys to see her eight-year-old daughter who refused to go to school or leave the house at all. Glenys prayed hard about this – how would she communicate with the child? She felt that God asked her to tell the story of David and Goliath. How strange! Glenys did her best to involve the little girl in the story and soon she was agog.

Shortly afterwards the girl's mother phoned and sounded delighted. 'We've had a breakthrough – she's been to the pantomime!' The child had identified Goliath in the story as her fear and saw that she had to overcome it. Soon she was back at school and living quite normally again. Abuse had not been an issue, and yet how easy it would have been for Glenys to jump to the wrong conclusions, making the situation a hundred times worse.

Slow but sure

Abuse can cause all sorts of problems in adults. There is not the space to write very much about this complex subject, but several good books on it are mentioned in the Appendix.

When it comes to those who have been abused, counselling takes time. Often the abuse has remained hidden and festering for years, and suddenly the monster is out in the open. The survivor's whole view of life has been distorted from childhood. They see everything differently from the rest of us.

Foolishly, many churches expect them to become whole after a week of counselling, but this is unlikely. People simply do not appreciate the extreme trauma involved. If a child's parents, brother and sister had been killed in a plane crash which she herself had only just survived, would we expect her to 'get over it' in a few days, even with professional help? If the trauma was not worked through at the time, the damage it caused might well surface in adulthood. In the case of abuse, foundational things have been destroyed, like self-worth and the ability to trust and to relate properly to others.

It is helpful to be honest with the client – to tell her that it may take years before she has worked through all the issues involved. This does not mean only the abuse itself. She has to adjust her view of the world and how she acts towards others. She may feel much worse before she gets better.

Though an experienced counsellor can be extremely helpful, friends, especially in the church, have a tremendous part to play in showing tender loving care. In the meanwhile, although the survivors may need a great deal of help and support, they can make a real contribution. For example, Glenys talks about the poetry which some of her clients have shown her. The words are inspiring and flow from a place deep within.

We do see people come through to the place where abuse no longer dominates their lives, but sometimes the process takes so long that the person wonders if they will ever come out of the mess. Whether any become totally whole this side of heaven is open to debate, but then is anyone whole? All of us are products of brokenness to some degree. We all walk with limps, and helping people towards wholeness may not be the main aim of the Christian counsellor. In fact, abuse survivors can tend to think that everyone else is fine and that they are the only ones who suffer from damage. They need to know that the rest of us are not entirely whole either.

Some pointers in counselling abuse victims

First of all it is vital that people who have suffered sexual abuse are counselled by someone of the same gender. Because the abuse has often been locked away for a very long time before the person comes for counselling, one of the first steps is to create an atmosphere in which she can talk and the counsellor can listen. This is where we find the residential side of our counselling work so beneficial. It can take a couple of days before a client feels safe and accepted and able to speak about herself just as she is, without feeling that anyone has any expectations of her.

'I can't believe I'm actually talking about real things, instead of what I think you want to hear. It's like I've been wearing a mask for ever, and now I've taken it off!' sobbed one client in relief.

'You cry, now! Cry all day if you want,' said Glenys.

At that the woman smiled through her tears and said, 'I feel safe here. I know we're going to make progress, even if it takes time!'

Another woman, Kirstie, came all the way from Newcastle to see Glenys with her counsellor because they were stuck on an issue concerning abuse. Kirstie spoke so fast and in such a strong Geordie accent that Glenys did not understand a word. She sent up a quick prayer and either Kirstie toned down her accent or Glenys managed to interpret it, for they managed to communicate and sorted the problem out. Afterwards Kirstie turned to her own counsellor and pointed at Glenys. 'If *she* hadn't understood my first sentence I'd have walked out through that door!'

Another young woman, Rita, had been abused as a child and then was brought up in care. Because of her behavioural difficulties, she had ended up in a remand home. By the time she saw Glenys she was living as a single mother and a church had made contact with her through door-to-door work.

'Rita looked like she'd never been loved,' said Glenys, 'and she asked all kinds of things about me and my faith – quite suspicious, she was. And then, when she felt safe with me, she began to talk.'

Her language became more and more vulgar, for she had no other words with which to express her feelings and experiences. Glenys knew better than to judge her by the standards of middle-class Christianity and they made good progress. Rita had travelled a long way to see her and eventually Glenys managed to find a counsellor nearer Rita's home. This woman gave Rita hope, for she had also been abused and taken into the Local Authority's care, and yet she had come through to feel quite secure within a stable marriage.

If it is important for the client to trust the counsellor, it is equally vital for the counsellor to believe the client. The media have focused attention on false memory syndrome. Such problems may arise where certain forms of therapy are used – hypnosis, for example, or where the counsellor suggests or implies to the client that abuse has taken place. But in our experience people simply do not hallucinate or fabricate tales about being abused, and many cases we have handled have been proved in courts of law. Of course, if you ask any two people to describe an event they have both witnessed, each will give a different interpretation. An adult remembering things from her childhood may get a few details wrong. Why, though, would someone go through all the trauma of talking about terrible experiences if they never happened? Something would be very wrong with anyone who did that. That person would need help.

The far greater danger is for the counsellor not to believe the survivor. As well as having a history of not being believed, she may have buried her own agonising memories so deep that she finds it a real struggle to access them.

One woman who had been badly abused told Glenys, 'I somehow found the courage to go to the police station when I was a child, but the desk sergeant said that if I ever mentioned such a wicked story again, he would have me locked up!'

Another woman began her first interview with Glenys by stating flatly, 'I don't know why I've come, because you won't believe me – no one ever has.'

'I'll believe you, love,' Glenys assured her.

We have met people whose churches have forbidden them to talk about such things. They seem to take a 'head in the sand' attitude, either refusing to acknowledge that abuse exists at all or feeling that to mention it would somehow untidy things and contaminate everyone. The result is that churches – where of all places the captives should be free – actually contain people who can't say the word 'Father' or who freeze when a man approaches them.

When Glenys first started counselling women who had been sexually abused she felt in some ways inadequate.

'I'm sorry – I have no way of understanding what you

feel like,' she admitted to one client, and was surprised when a look of relief crossed the woman's face.

'Does that mean you won't give me the usual pat answers?' she asked.

The child within

Glenys prayed a good deal and she felt that God helped her empathise in a special way with the women who poured out such horrific stories. She began to see that many of them had something in common – great holes in their memories of childhood, with as many as eight years cut out of their lives. They felt as though a child locked inside them wanted to get out.

Glenys is one of those people who felt quite grown up from about the age of ten! Nevertheless, she sensed that God was asking her to help these women get in touch with the pain of the child within them. She found that progress could be made when the adult identified with her own suffering as a child. Only later did she read various books which confirmed this theory.

An adult can bring a new understanding where a child's perceptions have been warped. Lies can be put to rest. Many perpetrators push the blame onto the child, saying things like, 'You're so pretty, you made me do it!' The adult has believed this for so long that it can be difficult to see the truth.

Glenys asks sometimes, 'How old did you say you were when the abuse first happened? Six? Well, if I opened the door and brought a six-year-old girl in here and told you that her father had been abusing her, who would you say was to blame?'

'Her father!' the woman invariably replies, without hesitation.

'Well, can you tell me what's different about you, then?'

'Oh, but you didn't know me when I was a child,' the woman will often mutter, and it is necessary to press through until she sees the truth of the situation. How can a six-year-old be to blame for an adult man's illegal actions?

If an adult survivor can extend a sense of compassion for the child she once was, she stops hating herself and her whole personality begins to come together.

Often the survivor feels bitter that the adults who might have been expected to protect her at the time, failed to do so, for whatever reason. It can be helpful to see herself as an adult protecting that child who is still hurting. She can learn to accept and love and nurture the child within. That child needs her help because she has never grown up. She is stuck, emotionally, at the age when the damage was done.

If this happens the woman can regress temporarily. She may find herself laughing at inappropriate moments or otherwise behaving quite childishly. In attempting to run from their inner pain, many have made their lives exceptionally hectic. They may need to take time aside from a busy work or family life to express some child-like behaviour.

One woman, when alone, allowed herself to say, 'OK, kid, let's play!' In this way she made up for some of her lost childhood, and she became quite adept at fitting such times into her normal routine. She smiled, though, as she told Glenys of how she was standing in a supermarket queue one day. 'I felt an urge to go to the toilet and realised that I was squirming about and crossing my legs, just as a little girl might,' she smiled. 'And then I thought, "For goodness' sake, you're grown up, you can hang on for a few minutes! It's not appropriate to be in touch with the child in you right now!" '

Sometimes the woman cannot identify with the child within her and always talks about her own childhood in the third person. In that case Glenys will ask her to share her memories. If she is a Christian, together they ask God

to heal those memories, but this is not as effective as when
the person faces up to and recognises the real place of pain
of the child within her.

Forgiveness

Many survivors, not surprisingly, find it hard to forgive
their abuser. They may struggle more generally with
forgiveness as well. If they belong to a church, and have
talked about their abuse at all, they are usually told that
forgiveness is a key and that if they won't forgive others,
God won't forgive them.

We all know bitter people. A lack of forgiveness does
terrible things to human beings. It is true that forgiving is
a vital step in an abuse survivor's journey towards healing.
However, we often see clients who want to forgive, but
can't.

Often a woman will say something like, 'I told my
pastor I had forgiven my father, but I haven't!' No one
can tell these people to forgive – it has to be a free-will
offering. It is as though they are on a journey. They can't
get on the 'bus' of forgiveness until they come to the bus
stop. This might be the place of revelation of God's
overwhelming love and forgiveness for them. Once they
have boarded the bus, as it were, and found the ability to
forgive, their progress speeds up. Often, after about a
month, we hear, 'I feel so much freer!'

Continuing support

After counselling, we often keep in touch with clients by
letter or phone and many return a few months later for a
second week. The client will often feel that she has left
sackfuls of rubbish behind at Barnabas House, but at the
same time she will be incredibly raw. Back home she will
need people around to care and pray for her, and to take on
something of a counselling role if possible. It is really
important that we liaise with her home church, so that they

give support rather than crush her under the weight of their false expectations of her overnight healing.

Incest

Incest is often a closed world, and though it may affect a family for generations, the problem may only be evident from the outside if the smallness of the genetic pool produces a number of human beings who are odd in one way or another.

Many people think that incest typically happens in socially deprived areas of our inner cities, but in small rural communities it may have been the norm for generations, and the whole community is often horrified when an individual is arrested. A specialist team may attempt to re-educate the village, but sometimes I feel that social work teams can be over-zealous, assuming that everyone involved is a dangerous paedophile. In my experience these people pose no threat to anyone's children but their own.

In recent years incest has received publicity rather than being hidden and never mentioned. Generally, children are more aware and are encouraged to talk, and all of these things strike a blow at the practice. In remote areas people have become better educated, which tends to have the same effect, because incest is no longer seen as the norm.

Related issues

Adult rape.

Gender issues

The whole area of gender and sexual discrimination has been called a political time-bomb and has already provoked major conflicts in both Christian and secular society. We have seen major changes in this country's laws on homosexuality and sexual discrimination. In the same way there has been great debate and in some cases radical change in the church over the place of women in ministry. All of this has come about because individuals and groups were prepared to campaign.

Sexual discrimination

I feel that sexual discrimination is an abomination, though I am very much aware that it remains part of our society, especially in the work-place. Women still find it comparatively hard to become lawyers, barristers, doctors or company directors. A number of women who have come for counselling feel discriminated against at work. Many are angry about the way in which they have been put down by their male bosses. I find this strange, because all of my Social Services directors were women and we always worked happily together.

In some churches, people are prevented from coming into positions of responsibility – not because they lack skills and abilities or moral strength, but simply because they are women. We in the church need to be more aware of the direction in which society is moving in this area and seek to lead by example.

Of course sexual discrimination can work both ways. For example, counselling attracts more women than men and I have heard men complain that they feel discriminated against, though admittedly the organisations in which this happens are few and far between. Those groups defending the female corner will not help their case by assuming that all men are authoritarian, beat up their wives, abuse children or put women down. Both women and men can be horrible, but that does not mean that they all are!

Each gender has its own qualities and is different, but each is equal in value to the other. It will not help to rob men of their masculinity. Instead we should appreciate both men and women and allow them to be who they are.

Homosexuals

Christians who counsel within churches and in the wider community will have to deal with many of the problem areas concerning gender, and these issues challenge our value base. One of the major areas which the evangelical church has to face up to in this generation is homosexuality. We need to distinguish between homosexual tendencies, practice and lifestyle rather than jumping to the conclusion that all of these are sinful.

As a counsellor I am not convinced that people are necessarily born homosexuals. From my time in secular social work and health care, I know that it is dangerous to suggest to young people that they could be gay. Teenagers develop their sexuality over a period of four to five years, during which they feel unsure at times about their sexual identity. If peers or others pressurise them at this point, they may be pulled into something which is not really what they desire long term. They tend to get sucked into a distinct sub-culture and the whole experience could affect them emotionally for the rest of their lives.

For some the process starts earlier – I believe that people can be affected by abuse or trauma in their childhood. Others may have been pushed towards homosexual tendencies by a sudden change in relationships, over-closeting or rejection by parents or key carers.

As a Christian I firmly believe that God has not made us to have homosexual relationships, but I also understand that this can be difficult for many. I feel that it is important to accept people for who they are and to try to help them in every way possible. However, if a practising homosexual does not wish to change, but sees his or her sexual practices as acceptable before God and others, then I am not in a position to give guidance or support with regard to the way ahead. Instead I would recommend that the person consider seeing a counsellor who specialises in this field.

It is more usual for Christians to come to Barnabas House saying that they are attracted to people of the same gender but do not wish to practise homosexual activities. They do not want to be involved in the Gay Movement or similar organisations, but often they feel under constraint from others to 'be who they are' and to 'come out'. Many have suffered considerable pressure from those in society who wish to rip apart their Christian beliefs or pull them into the 'Gay Christian Movement'. They may need counselling to help them work through some of these issues.

I feel that mainstream Christians have much to answer for too. I have already mentioned that a secular psychiatrist once commented to me that the church was good at saving sinners, but hopeless at rescuing its own. When I asked what he meant he replied that a number of his patients were ministers from evangelical or charismatic churches who had either stated that they were homosexual or had been found out. He felt that the church had treated them badly.

As I said in an earlier chapter, I too have come across many cases like this. I would agree that the Bible forbids any sexual acts outside of marriage – homosexual or heterosexual. Leaders who are involved in such things may need to step down from ministry for a time, because they need help and support. But it has saddened me greatly when men have suddenly been deprived of home, job and income – even when they have explained that their homosexuality possibly started as a result of childhood abuse and were asking for help. No support was given to them, no assistance to plan their future life. Christians believe that our God loves to reconcile and bring people back to himself, so why, I wonder, are many churches so uncaring?

One pastor I know preached against homosexuals for years – real blood and fire stuff – until the day his son confessed to having been a practising homosexual from his early teenage years. The pastor was devastated and so was his ministry. He, his wife and his son came to see me. It transpired that the wife had wanted a girl, not a boy, and had dressed her child for the first three years of his life in girls' clothes, suppressing his masculinity. After nearly a year's counselling we saw reconciliation and forgiveness. They were set free from things which had bound them for years. God's grace is powerful and sometimes he turns things round in an amazing way. The young man is happily married now and his parents, instead of persecuting the gay community, are working to bring God's unconditional love to them.

If Christians would become more caring and less dogmatic, I feel that many people would come to faith sooner. If we accept the alcoholic, the adulterer, the thief and even the child abuser, why do we fail to cope with those who have problems in the area of gender? We need a great deal more patience and love.

One of the first things I have to do as a counsellor is to learn to accept people as they are. I will get nowhere if I feel antipathy towards someone whose sexuality differs from my own. This is not always as straightforward as it sounds. I used to find conflicts within myself while counselling homosexuals, and when I came to look at my prejudices I realised that many of them originated, not from my Christian background, but from my time in Social Services. In the geographic area where I worked the management would not tolerate anyone with homosexual tendencies – an unusual state of affairs, but none the less true.

More and more homosexuals come for counselling at Barnabas House – male and female, most Christians, some from society at large. Over the past ten years the number who have asked for our help has surprised me. It is a greater issue than I had ever realised. Each comes because of a perceived problem; many because of a broken relationship. They have decided that this is the time to explore and discuss the wider issues. The counsellor must remember that this person has lost someone very dear and will be experiencing as much grief and loss as someone going through a divorce. Often these areas of grief must be looked at before considering sexual orientation.

The first thing I will want to establish is acceptance. I have found that many experience guilt about their feelings when there is no reason why they should. Secondly, I will help homosexuals to explore their personal pain. Thirdly, I will look at their relationships and thought-processes. Then I will help Christians explore their relationship with God and with the Christian community. They need to recognise that God loves and accepts them for who they are. They are not odd or peculiar, but they are going through conflicts of emotions and identity.

Many who still have homosexual tendencies have stated that they do not wish to continue in that scene but to find a new way ahead by remaining celibate and becoming part of a loving and caring church. I try to encourage these clients to walk a road where they feel in control, for I believe that there is healing, peace and restoration in the gospel of Jesus Christ for those who wish to take that road. I have seen a large number go on to keep the faith, remaining celibate but establishing good, meaningful relationships with both men and women.

Relatively few may be restored to heterosexuality and marry happily ever after. Anyway, marriage does not necessarily prove freedom or wholeness, nor should it be seen as the milestone of success and 'normality'. Celibate homosexuals, along with anyone who remains single within the church, need to feel loved, valued, special and a part of the family. It is up to the church to accept people for who and what they are.

Transsexuals and transvestites

One day I was called to a hotel where a man had died of a sudden heart attack. It was discovered that he was a minister of religion, but four or five times a year he took himself off for a short break and dressed as a woman. That was how his body was found.

His family and church were devastated. His wife said to me, 'Now that he's dead I can't ask him why he needed to do this.' I felt sad that such a troubling question was added to her grief at that time.

I am aware that in certain geographical areas transsexuals and transvestites are associated with open debauchery, but that is not the kind of message I pick up from those who come to us. They are hurting and confused people who need to be accepted for who they are. Both the church and wider society can be so judgemental, fearing that these people are some kind of threat. Perhaps that is why more and more of those who are unhappy about gender issues come to a Christian counsellor, who will offer them unconditional regard and allow them to discuss their personal pain and problems.

I find that many lack a sense of identity in the area of their sexuality, and this often stems from negative childhood experiences. Transsexuals may have medical or anatomical problems. I try to have good medical help available, and also psychologists and psychiatrists where appropriate. The majority of those I see are not involved in sin, I feel, but need to accept their own identity. The Christian counsellor may be put under pressure to see these people change. Some will, though it may take a considerable time. Others will not, and I feel that we have no alternative but to accept them with love and compassion, as they are.

Gender problems are an extremely complex area, requiring skilful help. Granted that sin may take people in a certain direction over issues of sexuality, and granted that change can only take place as a matter of choice, in many cases there is an underlying deep hurt within. I do not see my role as counsellor as one where I will criticise, condemn or stand against those who are struggling with gender issues. Rather I would want to care for and love them as Christ loved us. One chorus I have found helpful when dealing with these matters begins, 'Jesus take me as I am, I can come no other way.' I know that as people draw nearer to God, there is always an opportunity for change.

11

Stress, Redundancy, Depression, Illness

Stress

I have mentioned stress in some earlier chapters, especially Chapter 1. Combating it has become a multi-billion dollar industry, complete with glossy image, but recent research has shown that much of our thinking on this subject has been wrong. Therefore, before entering into the whole area of stress management and control, it is important that all services offered are carefully analysed and researched.

Stress is a part of everyday life and we will all experience it at different levels at different times. I have sat through enough highly expensive courses which encouraged me to avoid stress by such means as placing my socks in a neat pair ready for the morning. To be honest, I quite enjoy a little stress to start the day as I ask my wife what she's done with my socks and then receive the usual rude reply. It wakes us both up!

The removal of all stress may cause serious problems – for example, research shows that people can become depressed, angry or withdrawn. If the counsellor is to help clients reduce their stress levels, he must do this gradually, or they may sink into depression.

187

While we all need some stress in our lives, obviously an excess of it can cause depression, breakdown and all manner of ills. Our society is very good at producing high levels of stress and in each individual the different contributing factors build up on top of one another in a kind of layering process. If this is not dealt with, breaking point may be reached.

Stress affects so many areas. Unfortunately I only have space here to write about a few of the issues which have struck me most forcibly in my work, especially with my Christian clients.

Over-work

I feel that some churches have a good deal to answer for in this area. As soon as a person comes to Christ, too frequently he or she is flung into all sorts of church activities. When I look back at my own experience I am horrified that within a few weeks I found myself teaching in Sunday school. Within a few months I was running youth activities all over the place. At the time I lacked any real foundation of who I was in Christ and my roots did not go very deep into his word or his ways.

Many Christians hold down a day job as well as performing various functions in their church. They attend numerous church meetings and involve themselves in worthy social activities as a form of 'outreach'. They can develop such a strong work ethic that when someone comes along and shares their vision to help homeless people, or to rise early and pray for hours, they try to take all those things on board as well. That's fine, if God has asked them to, but has he? If so, does he want them to give up something else? He knows we can't do everything.

Jesus said, 'The Son can do nothing by himself; he can do only what he sees his Father doing' (John 5:19). We know that Jesus did not take on board everything that people pressurised him to do, and yet we feel guilty if we say 'no', or if we ask to be released from one of our jobs! The fault may lie with us – for example we may feel secure and loved only if we are doing something. We pay the price when our family life suffers and our own time with the Lord is squeezed out.

Being a Christian is all about relationships: first with God, as the first commandment says, then with our family and then with others, including the church. I believe that many Christians have their priorities wrong because they are too involved with church activities.

Of course Jesus also said, 'If anyone comes to me and does not hate his father and mother, his wife and children . . . yes, even his own life – he cannot be my disciple' (Luke 14:26), but that is just one verse over a specific issue. God himself put people in families and Jesus knew about all the needs of people – physical, emotional, spiritual and relational. I find it interesting that if he wanted to say something important to his disciples, he often did it in the context of a meal, when they were all seated around the table in a family atmosphere.

Combating stress has a good deal to do with having our roots deep in a right relationship with God. If we know, *really* know, that even if we sit in a chair and never do another thing he will still love us unconditionally, then we will be free to find his perspective. In other words we will be free to do only those things which we see our Father doing.

Among church leaders

I counsel many young ministers from the established churches who experience burn-out. They are expected to lead three services every Sunday, a deacons' meeting on Monday, the Tuesday prayer meeting, the Wednesday young church, the Bible study on Thursday, the youth meeting on Friday and the Saturday inter-church activity. In between they are run off their feet with complex

pastoral or administration issues, plus forward planning
and all the rest. A pastor who does not reach high standards in any one of these areas soon knows about it. At the
end of months or years of living at this pace, he wonders
why he is feeling depressed or why he struggles to relate
to his family.

At this point he may complain of over-work or undue
strain, but his superiors look back to similar timetables
which they endured as young men. Their attitude tends to
be, 'If we coped, why can't he?' Something similar happens to junior doctors who work ridiculously long hours in
hospitals. The consultants who are now in charge survived
the same thing, years before. No one considers that some
dropped out. Those who cracked up under the strain are no
longer around to make the decisions.

A doctor referred one national church leader to me.
We'll call him Fred. He arrived on my doorstep and stood
there as stiff as if he had been encased in a suit of armour.
We practically had to lift him into the house.

Fred had seen great success in fulfilling the world vision
God had given him. Colourful, outgoing and a great
orator, he was also deeply spiritual and in tune with the
word of God, but somehow his marvellous reputation had
overtaken him. His world vision, in taking off, had placed
too many demands on him. Speaking to a hundred leaders
in one country one day, jetting off to address 5,000 in
another continent the next – all this took its toll.

'They say they want me here, there and everywhere, and
insist that I have a special anointing of God on me. How
then can I say I need a day off?' he asked. 'If I do, no one
listens or seems to understand.' I knew what he meant.
Too often Christians, quite wrongly, look to the man. If
they are organising a big evangelistic rally they must have
Billy Graham or Luis Palau. I have observed that when a
talented music leader moves on from a church, half the
congregation may leave. It can happen even in our own set

up. If I fall ill and send another of our excellent trainers to
take one session of a course in my place, I know he does
just as good a job as myself. Yet course members and
church leaderships can become quite upset.

Fred's feelings of guilt had extended to the issue of
spending any money on himself, and worst of all he had
no one to talk to.

He explained, 'Do you know, Roger, the number of
times people say to my wife after a meeting how wonderful it must be for her – living with a man like me? They
don't know I'm in such a state that I can hardly speak to
anyone on a one-to-one basis any more!'

I have noticed that those who are gifted at addressing
big congregations often feel isolated or guilt-ridden in
themselves. So can musicians, comedians and other enter-
tainers from the secular world. Some find an outlet in
drink, drugs or sexual promiscuity. Fred led an honour-
able life, but the pressures on him had become unbearable.

'I can't go on any longer,' he whispered.

'You need to talk about the pain you are feeling,' I said;
'the hurt and guilt and frustration. Think through what is
your responsibility and what is God's. Everyone has
legitimate needs, you know! It looks like yours have
remained unfulfilled for so long that they are slowly killing you.'

I drew a map on a piece of paper. 'Now, Fred, imagine
you're driving a thousand miles down this motorway,' I
said. 'Would you do it without stopping at all?'

'No,' he replied. 'I'd need to refuel, have some breaks
for coffee and meals, relieve myself, maybe stop the night
somewhere.'

'Fine,' I said and drew in service stations at twenty-five-
mile intervals. Pointing to them, I continued, 'At the
moment you need to stop often. You must take at least
two days off every week, and I don't mean to study or
write books. Go out with your wife, play or watch your

favourite sport if you like. Do whatever you find relaxing, so long as it has no connection with your ministry. And you must explain to everyone that those two days are non-negotiable.'

This type of counselling could hardly be called non-directive, but right then Fred was not capable of making decisions. I informed his organisation that he would be taking time out and he worked with me for many months on a planned programme. As his stress decreased, my role became less directive and he began to take full control of his own life again. Sometimes it became possible for him to skip one of the 'service stations'. Today he is functioning well in his ministry. Fred has a real heart for people, but he has learned that if he is to serve them, he must consider his own needs as well.

God made all of us different. Some have a higher capacity for work than others. Some need less sleep, some thrive on pressure, some can handle several things happening at once. My friends joke that I have always managed about three full-time jobs at any one time, but we cannot put things on other people who may be made very differently from ourselves.

Jesus needed times of peace alone with his Father in the desert. At other times he enjoyed relaxing with his friends Martha, Mary and Lazarus. The Ten Commandments specify one day of rest a week, because God made us and he knows that we need it, yet for many Christians Sunday is their most hectic day! Churches must realise that people are more important than activities. They must also ask God what he wants and not go marching ahead regardless. Too often impressive-looking programmes leave valuable members of the Christian army dropping by the wayside. It can take years before those people function properly again.

Redundancy

For possibly the first time in living memory, the sudden loss of work is affecting all areas of society, including professionals. Architects and surveyors, accountants and bankers, lecturers and teachers, as well as people trained in various branches of the medical profession, often thought that they had jobs for life. When such people are made redundant in their late forties or early fifties, realistically most are unlikely ever to find similar work again.

The majority wait months or years before they seek the help they need as a result of the knock-on effect of their redundancy. In counselling I have discovered many who are angry or sad. Some are going through a real grieving process.

The financial effects on the whole family are obvious and some clients need help with money management. But on a deeper level, husbands often undergo a form of personality change. While still at work they function fairly well within their family and social life, but afterwards they find themselves becoming more aggressive at home and less tolerant towards their children, especially any adolescents. A husband may become jealous of his wife's career or active social life. He feels a loss of social status, but also a huge loss of self-esteem.

Many who are made redundant for the first time experience overwhelming feelings of loneliness and isolation. Even where, looking from the outside, I see their families functioning reasonably well, I have often come to learn of marital and other family problems. Some who become redundant experience serious depression or psychosomatic illness and even those who appear to cope well can feel fragmented on the inside. Their world has collapsed in little bits all round them and they suffer from just as much stress as those who are over-worked.

Redundancy appears to have exactly the same effect on Christians as it does on those from the wider community. In addition the church, certainly in this country, has a strong work ethic. St Paul said, 'If a man will not work, he shall not eat' (2 Thessalonians 3:10). When work is simply not available, Christians can feel extra guilty.

Some find a measure of fulfilment by throwing themselves into unskilled voluntary labour, through churches or other channels. Old ladies need lawns mowing, buildings need decorating. Others lack the physical or emotional strength to pick themselves up and start to do this. Christians often feel trapped because they believe that they would somehow let God down if they expressed their desperate feelings of loss and inadequacy. Talking about such things may not be encouraged within their church, but the counsellor can give clients permission to let those feelings out, and then offer positive help and support.

The counsellor can get the person to look at his sense of self-worth and help him to realise that he is still of value. Christians will begin to find that life takes on a more healthy sense of proportion if they really grasp that God loves them for who they are rather than for what they do – or do not do. From that point, they may well find themselves able to use time in a more positive way and start to feel themselves a whole person again.

Depression

It should not be surprising that this is the busiest area of work for many counsellors. There appears to be more clinical depression in this generation than ever before and it has become a major problem in mental health. Around 30% of people in this country will suffer an episode of it at some time during their lives and it is no respecter of a person's academic attainment or spirituality.

Statistics show that 20% of patients visiting a GP will show some form of depression.

What is depression?

It is used as a blanket word to describe a variety of unbearable conditions. We have all felt a bit 'down' sometimes, and we may tell people that we feel depressed, but the clinically depressed person feels totally unable to change and this feeling persists. He feels as though he has an illness. Life loses its colour and there is little motivation even to do common-place things, like taking an interest in his own children.

The depressed person can feel hopeless, inadequate and full of despair. He may lose the ability to concentrate or to sleep, will often feel great fatigue and have a variety of physical symptoms. He can become irritable and self-centred and not that pleasant to know. People's reactions compound his feelings of rejection and isolation. In the most severe cases the person may suffer delusions of guilt or persecution, and a Christian may become convinced that, as the worst sinner in the whole world, he is beyond God's help.

There is a whole range of causes and degrees of clinical depression, and we can only skim the surface here. I want to say something, however, because the whole subject is surrounded by myths, especially among Christians. Some believe that all problems affecting the mind are the work of demons. This is simply not true. On one level the brain is a complex organ of the body which, like any other, can experience illness. Though there is no clinical test for mental illness or for any form of depression, most of us should understand a little of what it means to have depression which originates from an organic illness – we will have suffered from it mildly following a bad bout of influenza. Many women experience post-natal depression, which is due, in the main, to hormonal changes.

About 30% of depressed people have an organic change or illness which underlies their condition. This can range from Parkinson's disease to strokes and from thyroid problems to epilepsy and seasonally affective disorder. The treatment here will involve treating the illness.

Other forms of depression are not apparently sparked by physical illness, though they may well result in bodily symptoms such as fatigue and insomnia. Sometimes depression starts as a reaction to specific life events, such as trauma or bereavement. The person has good external reasons to feel down, but simply cannot find the strength to climb back up again, long after the time when most people would have recovered. Underlying emotional problems such as suppressed guilt or anger, perfectionism or rejection, may prevent normal grief reactions. They may make the difference between the person who slides into depression, and his friend in identical circumstances who does not. The counsellor can often help the person to understand and to deal with his unresolved feelings.

Endogenous depression is not related to painful circumstances, but appears to come from nowhere and may be experienced at any age. Several generations of one family may suffer, in which case it could be said that they have a genetic predisposition towards it. A person may experience extremes of highs and lows – manic depression – or else episodes of depression interspersed with periods of 'normality'. Short-term medication often improves things quickly, especially for those who suffer from endogenous depression. People tend to be suspicious about anti-depressants, but they work effectively for more than two-thirds of those who take them.

It is important that anyone suffering from any of these forms of depression should see a doctor in the early stages. Unfortunately, the condition is seen as shameful, whatever its cause. Many are reluctant to ask their GP for help, fearing that they will be classed as lesser beings. Most

Christians are worse and feel that to consult a non-Christian doctor is a real admission of failure. Christian circles often give the medical profession a bad press, but most of their prejudice stems from profound ignorance and an unwillingness to find out more.

A counsellor, Christian or not, must be prepared to work alongside the medical profession and know enough to be aware of when a client needs his doctor's help. I expect my clients to follow their doctor's advice and to continue with any medication they are prescribed. The counsellor still has an important role, in coming alongside the person in his pain and offering hope. He may also help a depressed person to evolve ways of coping with life. Obviously if the person is experiencing extremely severe symptoms, such as hearing voices, having delusions or being completely unable to sleep, these things may make him inaccessible to counselling for a while.

Positive and negative thinking

Depression affects different people in different ways at different times. It may help sometimes to say, 'It's a wonderful day, let's go out and do something to take your mind off it,' but often such a suggestion will make the person feel worse. The last thing he needs is bouncing by Zebedees – although at times positive thoughts or actions may prevent him from spiralling lower.

Research shows that those people who talk about their deep emotions, such as guilt, anger, resentment or rejection, can prevent damage later in life. Some Christians, though, teach that it is wrong to express anything negative. We should instead focus on our glorious inheritance in Christ and pray or praise our way out of any dark cloud.

Of course on one level positive thinking can be healthy. Suppose I sneeze or my throat feels a little dry. If I start to worry that I am going down with a cold, my thoughts spiral downwards. This may well depress my immune system and I might as well start buying bulk supplies of Kleenex. If I carry on working as normal, I may well escape – or so the theory goes. On the other hand, experience tells me that positive thinking, and even prayer, is not always going to prevent me from catching a cold.

Certain teaching implies that in Christ we are always on top, living glorious, colourful lives, with never a problem, never an illness. Anything less than that means we have let Satan in. Anyone who receives such teaching and falls short of its ideals can feel that he has let down God, his church and probably his family as well. If a church member is unfortunate enough to suffer some physical illness which causes depression, or to have a family history of mental illness or melancholy, he can be forced by the church into a position of denial. 'The world is wonderful, life is great,' he is told – but it isn't. He feels terrible, he feels hurt, but he is not allowed to say so. If he does open his mouth, some well-meaning person will thrust one of a selection of 'appropriate' Scripture verses down his throat, as though he were a slot machine programmed to produce a neatly-wrapped chocolate bar of happiness. He may have heard the verse so many times before that he will not really listen. Even if he does, he may not at that stage be capable of appropriating the truth of the words for himself. If his suppression of real feelings continues, sooner or later he may collapse in a breakdown.

Counselling depressed people

A counsellor can offer a safe place to such a person. The key will be unconditional acceptance. Once the client realises that he is accepted as a person unconditionally within this relationship, he can find release in pouring out his feelings. This is not the time for the counsellor to offer help, advice or Scripture, but to listen to the client's pain and despair and find out where he is at.

The danger is that we live in an instant society. We splash hot water onto powder and within a few seconds we are eating mashed potato. We use credit cards to enable us to buy what we want – now. Then we look at Jesus, who appeared to heal people instantly. We try to do the same, but often we merely cover a person's deep wounds in order to make ourselves feel better. I do think that prayer for depressed people is effective, but I make it clear to the person and his church that I do not expect immediate results. Once the person has worked through his pain, then prayer and truth from Scripture may start to show their effectiveness.

With depression a time process is involved – at least six to twelve months. I have known it take up to three years before someone shows real signs of improvement. The person needs time to explore his feelings, to learn to be who and what he is. If he feels low or sad, that is acceptable. Adding guilt to the mix will not help.

Imagine a man lying on the floor. Someone throws a sheet over him. If he is healthy he can throw it off easily. If his arms are paralysed or he is very weak it may prove more difficult. If someone adds ten heavy blankets, there is no way he can push them off on his own. We have to help him remove the blankets one at a time. If we do this too quickly with a depressed person, he may spin into a state of anxiety.

Jim was referred to me by his health authority. He had been depressed for three years, and many others in his family suffered from acute depression. The health authority also referred him for stress therapy, and I too felt that this might be helpful. However, on Jim's third visit the psychotherapist phoned to ask if I could come round to her stress clinic. Apparently Jim had made her so stressed that she could no longer cope!

When I arrived she was red in the face and perspiring profusely. Both she and Jim were very angry. Apparently she had got the group to lie on the floor and think beautiful thoughts about blue skies and bluebirds. Most of her clients found this peaceful, relaxing and helpful. However, Jim was a miner and used to strenuous physical work. He was also very involved in athletics. The inner conflicts created by the 'peaceful' stress therapy were so great he could lie there no longer. He had to stand up and yell.

'I never want to see a blue sky again!' he spluttered. 'And what's a bluebird anyway?'

I took him back to my house and we started walking around the garden. Immediately Jim picked up a shovel and started moving some chippings which were lying ready to be put on a path.

'I needed to do that,' he said, when he finally sat down with me over a cup of coffee.

Jim was not able to relax physically at the stress clinic, nor to cope with the cognitive thinking processes employed there. I felt that running would provide a more appropriate form of relaxation for him, although it was important that he did not overdo it and become exhausted. He was not working down the mine at that time so we planned a programme which involved some running and also a limited amount of physical work.

I found out also that Jim felt particularly frustrated and down when attending his church and small house-group meetings. He could not cope in closed environments and felt very guilty because church increased his stress and depression rather than helping him. He suggested to me that he should stay away from all church meetings for some weeks. This became months, but he did not lose his faith and always wanted me to pray for him in counselling. Jim did recover and is now fully involved in his church and in Christian work.

I feel that the main role of the counsellor is to come down to where the depressed person is; to take time simply being there with him, listening, accepting him as he is, not saying anything except to show that we understand. The reassurance that someone else loves and cares is important. After all, we would spend time with a person who had a deformed leg. We would accept him and help him all we could rather than rejecting him because his leg failed to straighten as we prayed.

It can be hard to stick with a client who is very depressed, but it's amazing when he starts to recover. One man I had been counselling over a long period recently made my day by telling me, 'I've been for a walk in the park. It was wonderful. There were ducks on the pond!' He had been to that park each day for the past year or so, and would sit by the pond, staring blankly into the distance. He could have been anywhere. For him to notice the ducks was the first sign of a real breakthrough!

In long-term depression, carefully planned programmes play an important part in recovery. I ask the client to consider what he could possibly change in his lifestyle. If he has been depressed over many years, he may at first feel that it is impossible for him to change anything, but I encourage him to explore every area, such as work, home and finance. Once he begins to understand that change could take a long period of time and that he need not feel guilty about this, he may be on the road to recovery.

Sometimes he has lost touch with normal family life, so I will often try to involve family members, for example getting them to discuss what small thing my client could do around the house or garden which would not prove too stressful, but which would bring him a sense of achievement, confidence and involvement.

I will also ask him about the skills he possesses in the areas of art or craft, of design or writing perhaps. He may have forgotten about these, but they can provide gentle, positive targets to help him through some dark periods. If he is involved in a church, I will ask him about that too. Often I find that those who suffer from depression sit through meeting after meeting feeling awful. There seems little point in this, so I will encourage them to talk about how they feel about the meeting with their pastor.

Of course some people would not need the services of a counsellor if their churches had dealt with them more sensitively in the first place. Churches where people are encouraged to talk and share about themselves in a supportive way, however, do a tremendous amount of good. The house-church movement and cell groups in other churches have pioneered some helpful models for this. People who are already depressed often find their healing more quickly in such an environment. And yes, it is scriptural to share weaknesses, problems and sins as well as joys and strengths – the Bible calls it 'carrying one another's burdens' (see Galatians 6:2). For what is the role of the church if not to heal the broken-hearted and set the captives free?

Suicide

Those people who are beginning to emerge from depression are perhaps the most likely to commit suicide. Over 4,000 people a year in Britain take their own lives, and it is important that a counsellor takes seriously any indication that suicide is likely. Opinion varies as to whether counsellors should continue to take a non-directive approach in these circumstances. Wherever there is a life-or-limb situation – in other words where a client is likely to hurt himself or someone else – I myself switch to a more directive approach. I feel that I do have some responsibility for my client, so I will give guidance and actively try to prevent harm from happening. I would direct the client towards other professionals, such as doctors, psychiatrists or – where the abuse of alcohol, drugs or other dangerous substances is involved – towards specialist rehabilitation units.

Depression among leaders

If leaders are against church members talking about their emotions I usually find it is because they suffer from deep hurts in this area themselves. 'Don't come near me,' they seem to say, 'or you may find out what I'm like. You won't want to know me then.'

It has been said that depression is the padre's Achilles' heel. By the time they come to see me, leaders and pastors are often in the acute stages. Sad to say some are looking for further help after being treated in a rehabilitation or mental health unit. Others are in desperate need of medical help. Many come from charismatic churches which deny completely that depression can form a part of everyday life.

If leaders work as part of a team among whom they can share any of their feelings in honesty and openness, I find that they are far less likely to suffer from depression. Others who work alone and carry huge responsibilities are often so busy that they have no time to develop any relationships, apart from shallow, activity-based ones.

One man from a traditional church background came to Barnabas House for counselling. A respected Bible teacher and theologian, he announced that he wanted to talk to me because he knew that I would not tell him to read the Bible or to pray. That left me wondering wryly just what he had heard about my work!

All I said was, 'I'm happy to give you some time.'

Then this well-educated man, dressed in a suit, came out with every swear-word I had ever heard – plus a number which were new to me – and that was quite an achievement considering I had spent years working with deprived adolescents! As the torrent continued to pour forth in my front room, I sat back and wondered, 'Lord, what do I do?'

'Don't worry,' I felt God answer. 'I'm quite secure in who I am, and I've heard it all before!'

After about forty-five minutes, the man started to weep. Sobbing, he asked for forgiveness. 'It's terrible what I said!'

We prayed together. He came to realise that God loved him and cared about him no matter what he said or did. He understood too that I was not shocked or upset, but accepted him for who he was. Now much calmer, he started to tell me of the pressures he felt, of the expectations which were put on him by his church and about his adolescent children who had sparked dreadful criticism and conflict when they turned up at services wearing jeans. He had been told that he should not be a leader because of this. The pressure had built up and up, with no opportunity to let it out until he came to me and started swearing so dramatically.

After that we were able to progress to a more conventional counselling situation. I saw him six times altogether and today he is functioning well. Sometimes I meet him at conferences and he puts an arm on my shoulder. 'Did I really say all those things, Roger?'

'Yes, you did!' I smile. It's wonderful to know that God understands.

It is not only leaders in the church who suffer from depression. Many professionals in the wider community also feel isolated emotionally. Good at giving out to others, they often hide what they really feel about themselves, and will not let anyone close to them. If social work directors can suffer in this way, counsellors need to beware the same pitfall. Of all the problems we deal with, depression is the one which is most commonly transferred to the counsellor. He will be in for the long haul, listening week in, week out to those who are full of

negative emotions. They may affect him before he realises it.

I feel that an hour is quite long enough for each session
and afterwards I try to take half an hour's break before I
see the next client. During that time I go off and do
something else. Counsellors also need people with
whom they can share their own inner pain. This is particularly important for those who have clients suffering
from long-term depression. If we find we can no longer
enjoy a sunset or a good film, we must pull away and talk
to someone. It is vital that counsellors have a life of their
own where they can enjoy themselves away from the
burdens of others.

Illness

Often people come to see counsellors because of a physical illness – perhaps to talk about their fears and worries.
The situation has become worse since the government
changed the rules on disability allowances. Those people
who are no longer able to continue in their previous
employment – due to a bad back or depression, for example – are now individually assessed. Many are told that
they are no longer eligible for the allowance and must find
work, and this can prove a huge pressure.

Where a child is seriously ill, parents or grandparents
can value the opportunity to talk things through, for it will
affect the whole family. I was once called to a police
station to help interview a young girl who had been
caught out soliciting. After some time the WPC and I
realised that this was the first occasion and that the girl
had not been successful in her attempts. Breaking down in
tears she explained that a charity had raised the money to
send her mentally retarded brother on a holiday of a
lifetime. She felt torn. On the one hand she was delighted
because she loved him, but on the other she longed to go

too and there was no way the family could afford it. Then she watched a television programme in which a group of sixteen-year-old girls were bragging about how much money they could earn through prostitution, and she decided to try it.

Her story had a happy ending. Social workers got together with the police, fire and ambulance services to organise a football match. All the years of aggression between the various sides found expression on that field. The rules were abandoned, the referees gave up, a wonderful time was had by all . . . and we raised enough for the whole family to go on holiday.

I find it sad, though, that in many cases where someone is seriously ill or handicapped, the needs of the rest of the family can be forgotten, even by people who are trying to help.

Illness is another area where Christian myth reigns supreme. A number of things are thrown at Christians who are unwell. They are told, 'It's all caused by the devil!' or that if they only had more faith they would be made better again. So where does that leave faith-filled men like David Watson or Roger Price, who died despite much prayer? As a counsellor I have to deal with the result of emotional damage caused to people who are ill. Well-meaning Christians, especially those from the 'faith' or 'prosperity' movements, often fail to take into account the personal pain of those who are not healed. So do enthusiastic preachers at evangelistic healing meetings.

I do believe that God heals sometimes, but there again sometimes he does not. I would not like to judge why some die while others recover. The statistics from any cancer ward will show that those with no religious faith at all can make an apparently miraculous recovery, flying in the face of the doctors' gloomy prognoses. Others with less virulent forms of the disease can die quickly. In some cases psychological factors, such as a positive attitude, play a part. Others remain mysteries.

If someone is ill, my job as a counsellor may include reassuring him that it is not his fault. I may need to help people to face dying in a dignified way, and to help any who are Christians prepare to meet God.

ME

They say that the ME sufferer is to the counsellor what gall bladder patients are to the surgeon – we see large numbers of them. Over the past fifteen years I have seen lots of people with ME. Some were suffering from rejection and consequent depression because important people in their lives refused to accept that they had a real illness. Though I am no expert, my own opinion is that ME does have a physical cause. It can start as the after-effects of a virus, or as the result of being let down, or of some sudden shock or failure. As the term 'yuppy flu' indicates, it can also happen to those who push themselves too hard. Unfortunately, the medical diagnosis of ME is often missed in the early stages, resulting in people getting worse.

ME brings with it aches, pains and extreme debilitation, resulting in the inability to cope with everyday life. This in turn brings lack of motivation, plus feelings of isolation and depression. Many sufferers also feel guilty and misunderstood, especially Christians. On the other hand the acronym ME can be appropriate as many sufferers become 'me'-centred. For them the rest of life might as well not exist. It has to be recognised that a whole family can find it terrible to have a member suffering from ME.

The good counsellor or pastor works hand in hand with the medical profession. I find the advice and support of a client's doctor invaluable in cases like ME where medical issues are involved. Together we can agree a series of goals and targets with the patient, in addition to plans for help and support.

The earlier someone can be encouraged to talk the better – for example, does he know what is triggering the process? It would help if his church released someone to draw alongside the sufferer, which will not happen if all the strong ones are overwhelmingly busy with worthy activities!

One woman, though attractive and well educated, was in a terrible mess when we first saw her. So debilitated that she could not lift her head, she felt as though she lived in a fog, and her self-image was so low that she had decided she had nothing to offer. It was important that I as a counsellor gave her permission to feel as she did without expecting anything of her. She obviously needed time to adjust her lifestyle to her unaccustomed tiredness. After many months of sharing and listening, she began to gain more confidence in herself. Her understanding family and church gave her excellent support. Today she is fit and well and active in her church. This is not unusual. In my experience, given time and space and someone to talk to, the majority of ME sufferers get better in a few years.

12

Loss, Bereavement, Trauma, Disaster, Mental Illness

Loss

One of my most interesting counselling sessions ever was with a missionary doctor who had worked all over the world. He said that he wanted to see me on a one-off basis to talk about an area of loss in his life. At the start of the session we prayed together and he began to cry. I could see that he was grieving about something very important to him.

'You'll probably find this the most ridiculous thing you've ever heard,' he said to me at last. 'I've lost my coat. I left it in the back of my car while working in a hospital a few days ago, and when I came back it had been stolen.'

He went on to explain how special the coat had been to him. A group of homeless people had bought it to thank him for helping them. Though they lived well below the poverty line, they had clubbed together, given all they had and somehow raised £200. They bought a coat, but it wasn't any old coat. This was a thermal one, designed for use in arctic conditions, for they knew that the doctor was about to start work in a very cold region of the world.

'Knowing how much it had cost them, part of me didn't want to take it, but I was amazed by their generosity. It

was the most wonderful and thoughtful present imagin-
able, and now it's gone I feel devastated.'

'I can see that you really are going through a lot of pain
over this,' I said.

'I am. It's stupid because in one sense it was just a coat.
But something personal has been robbed from me and I'm
left feeling desperately unhappy – for myself, yes, but
more for the people who gave it to me.'

We spent the day talking, reflecting, listening. He told
me that I was the first person who had allowed him to cry.
He was a big man, and doctors aren't supposed to get
upset about things, are they?

At the end he said, 'Thanks for listening. I feel better. I
need to move on.' I never saw him again so I don't know
the end of the story – whether eventually he recovered the
coat or not – yet obviously he felt content to have used the
time and space to share his sadness over something so
simple yet so important to him. A counsellor may find that
a client needs help over the loss of something which at
first seems insignificant, yet to him it will be very personal
and his grief real and important.

In these times, one of the major areas counsellors have
to deal with is that of loss. We live in a temporal, throw-
away society of 'haves' and 'have nots' – and the 'have
nots' perhaps once had lots. A man who is made redundant can feel rejected because no one now requires the
skills he put so much effort into attaining. He may
conclude that he has lost all value as a person. Many
Christians struggle with their faith, asking, 'Why me,
God?' and professionals, especially, can become angry,
introverted or depressed. Their loss affects relationships,
especially those within the family. They also lose the
companionship and status in society that work brought
them.

When I left local government employment for full-time
Christian work my status changed immediately. Former

colleagues saw me in a different light, which was quite right and proper, but it unsettled me none the less. I felt that I had lost the team with whom I had worked for years. I missed the opportunity of talking on a regular basis with other skilled professionals and the guaranteed access to certain resources. I missed the coffee and lunch breaks and the banter of the office. My new work has gone exceptionally well and I have an excellent team. God has been good to me and I would in no way wish to return to my former job, but, despite all this, it is interesting that I still felt some sense of loss.

Loss can come in many aspects. People who are childless or who never marry may experience an overwhelming sense of loss for what might have been. When we move house to a new area we may lose close touch with our friends and with everything which was once familiar, and we feel empty and rootless. The loss of physical or mental health, mobility, sight, hearing or independence may cause grief reactions as strong as those following a bereavement – whether these things happen to the person himself or to a close family member. With a divorce or separation the sense of loss and rejection is often reinforced by the pain of ongoing contact over access visits, financial settlements, etc.

Whatever the loss may be it can create acute stress and debilitation. If the person or those close to him recognise what is happening early on, it may ease the healing process considerably. It will help quite simply to know that someone else is walking the road with him. Scripture talks about wilderness experiences. That would be a good description of how those who experience sudden loss often feel: bewildered, lost, alone, dry, empty or even tempted maybe. People can find it helpful that Jesus went through such a time. Sometimes I point them towards passages in Isaiah which speak of a roadway through the desert, which can lead people out of the wilderness of loss to a new and fruitful start – for example Isaiah 43:18–19.

Bereavement

In some cases Christians, as well as those of other faiths and value bases, may have prepared for the death of a loved one, but however accepting they think they are, almost everyone experiences loss as acutely painful to body and mind. This distress may last over a long period of time, peaking as anniversaries and other reminders come and go. Few are likely to escape the normal process of feeling shock, unreality, denial, grief, depression, loneliness, guilt and anger. Bereavement carries with it all the intense pain of separation, even for those who believe that they will see their loved one again in a place where crying is unheard of. Since we still live on this earth, counsellors and churches must understand that Christians and those of other faiths need space and support as they grieve.

Bereaved people in distress often feel unable to approach their doctor or other statutory bodies, fearing that they will be seen as mentally ill. Friends and acquaintances may cross the road to avoid meeting them. These friends may be embarrassed and not know what to say, or may be afraid of emotion – either their own or the bereaved person's. In our culture, wherever death is still a taboo, bereaved people will feel isolated. Perhaps this is why more and more are coming to Barnabas House and other centres for counselling, sometimes years after the event.

In counselling they can talk about their long-term pain, or maybe their anger and desire to blame others. Grieving is a process that must be allowed to take place. Care and counselling have equal importance in providing safe places where individuals can talk about their anguish, or simply be aware that others are standing with them.

Different things can trigger distress and counsellors need to be sensitive to over-strong reactions to seemingly minor events. One lady came for counselling after her cat had died. It turned out that her husband had given her this pet three weeks before his own death, and the recent event had highlighted how sad and alone she felt. In another incident a girl was driving along the motorway when her radio blared out a news item about a fire. The details reminded her so vividly of an event in her childhood that she ran her car up the embankment, turning it over. Only the brave and prompt action of a passing lorry driver saved her life. Afterwards her church referred her to us for counselling.

Parents can be over-protective when someone in the family dies. Often they do not allow their children to go to the funeral. I have heard grown-up children regretting this years later, because a funeral is a good place to say goodbye. Sometimes I will encourage them to write a letter to the person who has died to give them an oppor-tunity to express what they wanted to say.

The church has tremendous expertise in working in the area of bereavement. Perhaps because it has been such a solace for many years, even in this generation many who do not claim to be Christians look to it for help and support at times of personal tragedy. They seek the peace and reassurance they cannot find elsewhere. As the church offers its services to the wider community I firmly believe that it should be seen as a place of warm acceptance, open to all those who need the opportunity to grieve and to share. As Jesus said, 'Blessed are those who mourn, for they will be comforted' (Matthew 5:4).

Comforting people may sound easy, but in my experi-ence bereavement counselling can prove volatile. Even the most sedate individual, with the strongest faith, will some-times curse and swear in the most appalling language. This is one place where such a person can safely let off steam. God understands and doesn't mind, so why should the counsellor? Should people's anger make them want to hit out, I encourage them to expend their energy on a soft toy or a cushion. Coming alongside people as they express grief may be difficult for the counsellor emotionally, but it is worthwhile.

For me, one of the most difficult areas in counselling concerns sudden loss, especially that of children. In Dickens' time and even up to the early 1950s a family might expect some children to die of TB or other diseases. Most of these are now cured by medical advances such as antibiotics. Today we see no reason not to hope for good lives for all our children. It shocks us when they are taken away, whether through illness or an accident. Over the past few years we have seen a number of children tragically killed in minibuses, canoes or other sporting misadventures. It is terrible when there has been no opportunity to say goodbye – if a child has gone to school or a husband to work quite normally in the morning, and died before the family sees them again.

Sudden loss is devastating for those who knew the person well, but it can also have a profound effect on a street, school or whole community. These people in the wider circle often receive little help, yet in many ways can experience as much pain as the family. Sometimes I have seen them in groups of five or six at a time and they seem to find this opportunity to express their feelings very helpful. At the beginning of this book I told the story of a young man who had been in my care and who committed suicide in prison. I vividly remember sitting down afterwards with groups of three or four teenagers at a time. Having known this lad at the centre where I worked, they needed to express their pain at his death and their anger about the system. They needed to ask questions, even if there were no answers. I gave similar opportunities to his other acquaintances from outside the centre, and they also appreciated this.

If the sudden death occurs as a result of a murder or suicide, the effect on family and friends will be even more traumatic. Many years ago I saw a client who was devastated because her husband had killed himself in his car by means of a hosepipe connected to its exhaust. He and the entire family were committed Christians and my client had been aware of nothing wrong in their relationship. Then, weeks after his death, she discovered from friends that her husband had been desperately unhappy with their marriage for the past twenty-five years. After his death she had no means of talking to him about the issues, which was a huge problem to her.

I set up a counselling scenario whereby she could speak to an empty chair as though her husband was sitting there. She allowed her anger, frustration and tears to flood out as she expressed her feelings. It took many months of counselling support and prayer after that before she could let go of her hurt and come through to start really living again.

I have also been involved in cases where a parent has been killed in a sudden act of terrorism, and another where the sexual abuse of a child has led to murder. Family members, and especially parents, feel immense anger, overwhelming sadness and loss, and sheer helplessness. Sometimes these things come out at the time, sometimes years later. I have found that it is always good to allow people to express themselves and to explore their feelings. In many cases this will mean an outpouring of abusive language which can on occasions be upsetting, especially when a counsellor comes from a Christian value base, but I see it as part of the counselling process. These people are only expressing their feelings in a safe and secure environment.

Commonly in such tragic situations family members hold themselves to blame.

'I made my son take that newspaper round!' one said.

'I knew something was wrong. I should have stepped in!' another whispered in shame.

'To think I encouraged my daughter to go out with that person!' another admitted.

In none of these cases were family members to blame for the tragedies. It is simply that those left to cope with the pain often take guilt on board. In this too they need help and support.

Tragedy can bring communities and churches together in a way they have never known before, with shared grief acting as a catalyst, even among people who thought they had nothing in common. I have been amazed by the kindness, love and gentleness of individuals, Christian or not, who give up many hours to comfort and to care at such times. Many individuals quietly give financial support at great sacrifice to themselves.

As a Christian, my hope and prayer for all I know who have been through bereavement, sudden or otherwise, is that one day they will see their loved ones in glory.

Related issues

Abnormal grief reactions. Caring for the dying. Dying at home.

Disaster/trauma

One Saturday afternoon in 1985 I settled down to watch football on television with the children in the assessment centre. Suddenly we saw live pictures which I will never forget. Flames were engulfing part of the Bradford stadium and a man ran across the field on fire. I prayed silently for him and for all who were caught in the inferno at that time. What else could I do? Though we were hundreds of miles away, the shock and sheer helplessness of seeing this event brought home how ill-equipped we are when major disasters or traumas engulf people's lives.

I have written in an earlier chapter about our involvement with a family who lost three of its members in the Kings Cross calamity. Even now, if a major fire is reported, they may phone, 'Just to see if you're OK, Roger.' They don't need counselling – just a moment to talk to someone who understands. Yet back in 1987 I felt so inadequate taking the funerals. Maybe some of my words there did help a few people a little. However, I realised that any love and care I could give the family afterwards would be far more important. I made a conscious decision that day to do my utmost wherever possible to offer counselling, care and compassion to those who struggle through times of trauma.

Over the past twelve years the team at Barnabas House, and myself in particular, have been working alongside those involved in major accidents or terrorist attacks. We see our role as working behind the scenes with the people and agencies who need support. For example, leaders of churches who find that a disaster has happened on their doorstep sometimes call on our expertise. I have to help them understand the major role which the emergency services play at such times. A whole cavalcade swings into action. Time will pass before churches are allowed to come alongside to help in the situation. Many find this frustrating, especially if they are a trusted part of the community or know the victims. The only thing they can do is to inform the powers that be of their availability and any expertise they have. Those who are wise enough to do this before a disaster happens will be in the best position to join the teams already working. Being local, their help in caring for individuals will be ongoing and invaluable, but even so, specialist skills are required in post-trauma work, and we need to know which aspects to leave to the experts.

It is essential in this area, perhaps more than in any other, that the counsellor shows the client unconditional respect and regard at all times. It is equally important that he has adequate ongoing supervision to help see him through his own personal grieving and close encounters with horrific circumstances, especially where children are involved.

At Barnabas House we give in-depth training in trauma work to all our staff and have made ourselves available free of charge to a number of emergency teams situated throughout the UK. We have helped people from Lockerbie, the Herald of Free Enterprise, terrorist attacks and other disasters – well known or not.

Despite the fact that the effects of post-traumatic stress disorder are widely understood, I am amazed at how little counselling is offered by the armed forces and others who should know better. Many who were involved in the Falklands or Gulf conflicts are now coming to us for help. We often find ourselves working with people whose personal trauma is surfacing six or twelve years after a serious road accident or other disaster, because they had no suitable person to talk to at the time.

I met an ambulance driver once whose area included the M4 and M5 motorways. He told me how helpless he had felt in failing to rescue a mother and child whose car went up in flames. Despite professional debriefing he could not get over his shock and anger at the fact that all his skill and training in saving lives had been of no use in this situation. Only after I had been counselling him for many months did he begin to come to terms with what had happened.

It is sad but true that those in the caring professions receive the least support in difficult times. In the past couple of years I have met many firemen, police officers and paramedics who have retired early because of stress and who are now asking for independent counselling from

Christian centres. Often, following extreme situations when they have no means of finding out what has happened to the people they have helped, their professional detachment cracks and they continue to worry. The cumulative effect of the appalling things they have seen has meant they experience continuous physical and mental pressure. Though their work-places these days often make good counselling available, employees hesitate to make use of it because of worries about confidentiality. If the fact that they have requested counselling goes on their records or otherwise leaks out, they fear loss of status and all chance of promotion. Their equals and inferiors would see them as wimps who could not cope.

Of course personal trauma does not always come in the form of headline-making events. People can experience similar reactions after separation or divorce, when their child or spouse is taken ill or after a road accident. They can feel traumatised as a result of a fire, flood, burglary or other crisis in the home – even one which is not life-threatening. Often we can forget the lesser things which put people into trauma and so fail to give them avenues to explore what has taken place in their lives.

At the other extreme comes a situation where a whole country or geographic area is in ongoing trauma. Many years ago I was invited to Northern Ireland to take a course on the subject of stress. When I found out that all of the thirty-eight people present had lost a close family member as a result of 'the troubles', I wondered what right I had to speak. Some of us from Barnabas House now travel to Northern Ireland around twice a month to work with families' who have lost loved ones. Referrals come to us through churches, doctors, solicitors and other agencies. Because of the delicate nature of the work we are unable to have direct contact with the emergency services, the police or army. Nevertheless, many from those fields who are traumatised and maybe struggling with alcohol or other secondary problems, find us through church settings.

People have found it especially hard to talk within the Province about the issues which disturb them the most. As Welsh people coming into the situation, we discovered that we could reach them more easily. Others preferred to visit us in Carmarthen to share their pain and grief. We found that many people from Northern Ireland have been unable to grieve, for a variety of reasons. Sadly, for many, grieving simply had no part in their culture or religion. Some religious people felt that since their loved ones had gone to heaven, showing any sorrow would mean letting God down. Others, whether Christian or not, turned to drink as a solace, or became involved in relationships which they regretted later. Ashamed of their reactions, they hesitated to ask for help and support. Guilt came in the way of others. Some felt so much anger towards the men of violence that they had no room for grief. Those of secular outlook often saw themselves as fighting an unseen enemy in a hopeless conflict which would never end. In order to keep up this mental state, like battle-ready soldiers they had to put aside their pain. In doing so they buried it so deep that they were unable to grieve cleanly, although in another sense life was a continual grieving.

There was a lull in the worst of the troubles after the Peace Accord was signed in October 1994, and we all hoped that it would be permanent. Soon after the immediate danger of hostilities subsided we found that people wanted to start talking about their own pain in a way they could not do while locked into the prolonged period of trauma. Many churches and secular bodies have now asked Barnabas House to become involved in more depth with the Province. We are planning a four- to five-year training programme to help these organisations deal with some of the issues arising from the troubles.

If my heart could be anywhere other than Wales it would be in Northern Ireland, for the most compassionate and loving people I have met in all the world live there – Protestants, Catholics and those of no faith at all. So many are breaking and hurting and yet they have been largely forgotten. I soon realised that those Catholics and Protestants with a deep and living faith in Christ were in fact better able to cope with the pain of these terrible events. They stood on firmer ground than those who had no religious beliefs. Many, though angry about what had been happening, longed for peace and reconciliation.

I have, however, seen people's faith tested to the extreme by violence perpetrated in the name of religion. It will need many years of help to restore their trust in a loving God who breaks down all religious barriers. I have noticed, though, that where someone has lost his personal faith as the result of some horrendous circumstance – and then regained it – he has become stronger. Some 'scar tissue' will remain all his life, and it is essential that he, and those close to him, recognise that his pain will return from time to time.

Wherever trauma has struck, I firmly believe that time is a great healer, but people need a safe place to talk about the things which trouble them. For many who have suffered trauma, in whatever circumstances, counselling and pastoral care will provide avenues whereby they can regain dignity and strength.

Related issues

Children in trauma. Murder and manslaughter.

Mental illness

This is not really the province of counsellors. They certainly should not attempt to label or diagnose people, but they do need to understand enough to know when to call in help.

Mental problems include anxiety states and phobias and obsessive compulsions – all of which can respond to a behavioural approach. Mental illnesses (such as schizophrenia or serious personality disorders) and affective disorders (such as depression) need psychiatric help, though counsellors may sometimes work alongside. Eating disorders – anorexia nervosa, bulimia and obesity – may also need professional help from psychiatrists or psychologists.

Even if someone has a serious mental illness such as schizophrenia, he will have periods of remission when he may feel that he is coping reasonably well. He may then seek out counsellors or other therapists, causing all kinds of confusion. That is why it is essential when setting up a contract with a client, or even when giving more informal pastoral care or listening support, to check if the person is seeing another professional. If he is, it would be wise to explain to the person the benefits of your talking to that professional, with his permission. The client or patient may see counselling or more informal caring as the answer to his problem, and it can look good in the short term. But should there be a relapse in his mental illness, professionals have to pick up the pieces created by well-meaning counsellors and carers. Because of this, many have adopted a scathing attitude towards counsellors, especially those involved in church work.

The other side of the coin is that professionals can be reluctant to talk to a lay person or counsellor or to give them the information they need in order to work properly in partnership to help the client. If we are to become more skilled and give better support to clients we need clear lines of communication between client, counsellors and other professionals who work in this area.

Other problems likely to be encountered

Aging-related problems

Middle age in men and women including the menopause and 'empty nest' syndrome. Senility. Sex and the elderly. Caring for the elderly. Elderly parents.

Inter-personal relationships

Communication skills, conflict resolution. Relationships in society.

Personality problems and self-esteem

Self-awareness, poor self-esteem, loneliness, anger, guilt, bitterness and unforgiveness, body image problems, rejection, domination by others, immaturity.

Religious beliefs

Spiritual abuse or harmful religious thinking. Religious cults, counselling for someone leaving a cult. Satanism and the occult.

Race and culture

Problems in immigrants. Cross-cultural counselling.

Social Services and the Welfare State

Understanding and liaising with Social Services, social security, probation services, prison services, legal services, voluntary services, eg Cruse, Relate.

Finances

Financial budgeting, debt, counselling for financial problems.

Addictions

Gambling, drug, alcohol or smoking dependency, addictions to stealing, etc.

Health education and lifestyle

Physical fitness, healthy and unhealthy diets, special diets, exercise, habit changing.

Sexuality

Sexual perversions, prostitution, masturbation, pornography. Sex and physical illness or handicap. Sexual problems in the female – frigidity, vaginismus; and the male – impotence, premature ejaculation. Contraception. Venereal disease.

Vocational counselling

The counsellor will need to understand and be able to analyse the personality types and how motivated a person is. Career guidance counselling. Changing careers in mid life.

The law

Counselling those who have been involved in crime or have been in prison.

13

Counselling within the Church

The demonic

Over the last fifteen years we have seen a massive increase in the area of deliverance ministry and in various models of inner healing. Names such as John and Paula Sandford, Steve Hepden, John Barr and Peter Horobin spring to mind. I know all these people well and they are excellent teachers who are always prepared to learn and to adjust their training should it be necessary. I firmly believe that there is a place for ministry such as theirs.

However, I see danger in the teaching which comes mainly from some evangelical or charismatic churches, when it suggests that everything that happens in a person's life is the work of a demon. I worry when people claim that there is a spirit for everything, whether it is depression, mental illness, sexual issues, dyslexia, or even woodworm in someone's house! One problem with this way of thinking is that it gives attention to the demons rather than to the power of our Lord Jesus Christ. Also, if people believe that every bad thing which happens to them is the work of demons, they are unlikely to take up any sense of responsibility. They may discount their own common sense and ability to change things, along with the professional skills of those who might be able to help.

By contrast, the counsellor deals with and respects the whole person and will want to give clients the opportunity to explore issues – to look at their past and present and their plans for the future. In counselling, a person can find the time and space to discuss his personal pain and the mistakes he feels he has made, and then consider how to make adjustments.

When working in the Christian arena, the counsellor can help the person to ask for God's forgiveness and to release his pain and worry to Jesus. Both counsellor and client can pray and expect to see God at work. Christians believe that there is such a thing as sin in the world, and that it is dealt with by repentance, through the cross. On the other hand, if we insist that a person has a demon of lust, for example, he may shift responsibility for his actions onto the demon and so is unlikely to repent and find God's power to change the way he thinks, lives and treats others.

If someone asks me whether a Christian can have a demon I would have to say that in the majority of cases I think the answer is 'no'. I do know of a few who have felt better after deliverance ministry. Only too often, though, I believe that the 'demons' which are cast out were never there in the first place. Here I would see deliverance as a form of spiritual abuse which can compound any problems the person may have had, whether these are related to stress, schizophrenia or an over-vivid imagination. Some who attempt deliverance throw themselves about and shout and yell. I see no evidence in the Bible for this. Demons are not deaf and neither is God, but the person might be if well-meaning Christians carry on like that! In certain notorious cases exorcists have shaken or jumped on someone so much that they have caused injury or even death. By contrast Jesus took authority over demons in a very calm way.

Occasionally, when counselling someone, I have seen signs suggesting demonic activity in them. It is said that if you try to counsel a demon, it will counsel you, so I have a very clear procedure for such cases. First I will ask the client if we can check his medical records. If we find that there are medical issues I will take appropriate advice. If not, and the person's behaviour patterns continue to cause concern, then I will terminate his counselling contract. This may seem harsh, but deliverance is not a part of counselling, nor is it dealt with in the training, so the counsellor will not be covered by insurance. To date no one has been sued for counselling in Europe, though sadly we may follow in the USA's footsteps one day. However, a man in Germany is serving a prison sentence for ministering deliverance.

Having terminated his contract I will recommend that the client seeks help from a church or ministry with appropriate experience and training in deliverance. After such ministry he will almost certainly need counselling again and I will then be happy to take him on with a fresh contract.

Prophecy and words of knowledge

A prophetic word or a word of knowledge is where God speaks through someone in a supernatural way, perhaps giving information or direction. I am often asked if I believe in such a thing. The answer is a cautious 'yes'. An earlier chapter describes how I came into my present work after three individuals, each unknown to the others, gave me almost identical words at separate times and places. Afterwards I spent much time praying by myself and with others, making sure that what I was about to do really was God's will for me. If I had launched forth earlier I doubt I would have been mature enough, and might well have ended up on an ego trip. It also has to be said that over the years, well-meaning individuals have given me 'words' about going to so many countries that if

I had obeyed them all, I would have spent my entire life whizzing about on aeroplanes.

The Bible says that we have to test the prophets. My problem with this whole area is that there is often no means for monitoring words of knowledge and prophecy. Over the past couple of years, I have seen a number of casualties resulting from them. In fact I think that words of knowledge can do more harm than the mishandling of deliverance, the 'Toronto Blessing' and counselling put together – especially where they give 'revelations' about sexual abuse, incest or marital issues.

For example, a lady called Linda came to see my wife once. A sensible, intelligent person, she confided a terrible secret to Glenys. A Christian woman, highly respected in the realm of spiritual gifts, had come out with the revelation that Linda's father had subjected her to sexual abuse.

'Apparently I was between six and eight months of age at the time,' explained Linda. 'But my conscious memories don't go back that far, so how can I know whether it really happened or not? If I doubt this woman's word I feel guilty and confused – and I hardly know how to look at Dad any more. Could he possibly have done this dreadful thing?'

Linda discussed all these painful issues with Glenys over a number of sessions. No real evidence of abuse emerged, but there did seem to have been some kind of trauma in early childhood. Finally Glenys asked if Linda felt she could talk to anyone about it. Linda had a good relationship with her mother. The only way she could find peace of mind was to take the brave step of asking her. Yet she knew that her question might damage the family beyond repair, even if the 'word of knowledge' turned out to be untrue.

Linda's mother just stared at her at first. 'But that's impossible!' she said finally. She and her husband had spent the first three years of their married lives on the mission field, but by the time Linda was on the way, the situation in the country where they worked had become very dangerous.

'So you were born here, Linda – you know that. Your dad stayed on the mission field for three whole years afterwards. Abuse from him would have been quite out of the question – or from anyone else for that matter. We lived alone, right out in the country. There was no one else around, and I certainly didn't abuse you!'

'Of course not, Mum!'

Still, something had happened in Linda's childhood, and her panic attacks did not stop. She talked further with Glenys and again with her mother. It became clear that for the first years of her life she had not been used to seeing many people other than her mother. When her father had returned from the mission field, although he loved her and there was no question of any form of abuse, she had been frightened of this strange man who came to live in their house.

Thankfully, through prayer and counselling, the situation was resolved. Her father, though angry at first, was a loving, mature Christian. They were able to pray together and this dear family was not damaged in the long term, but that 'word of knowledge', given with such authority, could have wrecked all of their lives.

I deal with similar situations on a regular basis and would advise anyone who thinks they have a word of knowledge to err on the side of caution. If it concerns matters such as abuse or marital infidelity I would strongly advise that they should not make any statement that such a thing has taken place. It would be very bad practice in counselling because it might well trigger false memory syndrome and thus bring the whole process into disrepute. In the case of a child who is still below the age of consent, words of knowledge concerning abuse should never be given. Anyone who gives such a word must be prepared to take full responsibility for what happens afterwards, and not hide behind a claim that they have heard from God.

I am not saying that all words of knowledge are incorrect, but tremendous damage has been done by those who think they have a hotline to God and rush to speak without first checking the history of the person and gaining as much background information as possible. Even if someone genuinely has heard from God it is important how and when the message is delivered. Once I counselled a man and felt something very strongly during our second session together. It did not concern abuse but something else which had happened in his life. However, I knew our relationship had not developed to the point where he would have been able to receive what I said. Not until our seventh meeting did I feel I could bring the subject up.

He told me then that I was quite correct, but added, 'Funny – if you'd have said that earlier, I'd have walked out!' In this case the word of knowledge proved useful as a short cut which helped us progress faster than before. Christian counsellors can and should listen to God, and they may find that he prompts them to start asking some gentle questions in a new direction. This is very different from coming out with an alarming statement of 'fact' and claiming divine inspiration for it.

Counselling post-Toronto

In February 1994, students on one of my advanced courses started telling me about some remarkable phenomena that were happening at their church, Holy Trinity, Brompton. Before long I became aware that this same 'Toronto Blessing' was manifesting itself all over the country. In Swansea and Cardiff thousands were gathering each week for special services – unusual numbers for Wales these days. Just as surprising, different denominations were being drawn to meet together.

When I went along to these meetings I took note of the kind of people receiving the blessing. Many had been my peers in the Elim ministry, or were known to me as leaders of other respected churches. I also recognised psychologists, lecturers and other professionals. I knew that these people were not normally subject to auto-suggestion, hysteria or excessive emotion, yet they spent most of the meetings prostrate on the floor or else kept making very unusual movements and noises. I felt totally confused when some of the most sane individuals I knew roared like lions, clucked like chickens or barked like dogs.

A man I knew came to pray for me and, without warning, I found myself on the floor. I thanked God that I did not seem to be making any noise. I simply lay there for two hours, feeling such peace in God's presence, and I had no doubt that something rather special was taking place. People call this experience 'resting in the Spirit', which is not a bad name for it. Other events in the room seemed to be verging on chaos at times, and the noise was deafening, but the meeting ended in an orderly fashion and again I took a good look around. So far as I could see everyone had regained their normal composure and none appeared to have been damaged or hurt by their experiences.

I went to several meetings where similar things happened. Much of it, I felt, was good, but I asked myself whether I wanted to belong to a church full of yelling, shouting, roaring and general chaos for the rest of my life. I wondered whether I, as a man of fifty-one, would have the energy to keep up with enthusiasts from a younger generation!

The media were showing a large amount of interest in the church's involvement with all aspects of the supernatural – from deliverance and inner healing to this new 'blessing'. Along with a television company and a Christian magazine, a number of Christian organisations requested that I visit the Toronto church where this phenomenon had started. They wanted me to give an opinion on what was happening in this 'Toronto Blessing', and what effect it was having on churches and families.

Two doctors from Belfast travelled with me to Canada. They share the same Christian name and are known as 'the two Ronnies'. In view of this, perhaps I should not have been surprised when the whole trip took on the zany logic of a comedy show. As a Welshman I could only feel confused when my itinerary said that I should fly from Cardiff to Belfast to Amsterdam – and then back over Ireland to Toronto in Canada. Apparently this was the cheapest route!

As we took off that day in January 1995 the two Ronnies told me that the Toronto church would be celebrating the first anniversary of the 'blessing's' arrival while we were there. We certainly found our hotel well prepared. Apparently, as people returned after meetings, its lobby was often littered with prostrate bodies or besieged by roaring lions! What had we come to, I wondered?

We found the Airport Vineyard Church almost at the end of the runway, in one of the most unattractive places I have visited anywhere in the world. The large, warehouse-type building seated around 4,000, but I found myself wondering why anyone would ever want to go there. Imagine my surprise when I found it featured in a magazine as Toronto's top tourist attraction – its visitors outnumbering those to the CN Tower or Superbowl!

At the first meeting the leader asked people from various countries to stand. Individuals had come from all over the world and I was impressed that out of the 2,000 or so present that night, those from the UK outnumbered the Canadians. In fact some immigration officials turned up at that meeting, because they could not understand why so many foreigners were arriving at the airport claiming that they had come to Canada in order to go to church. Having experienced part of the evening, those same officials left looking more confused than ever!

I began to understand at least one thing. Christian history shows us that revival usually starts in one place. Others travel to that place, take something of it back home with them, and so it spreads. This has happened with the Methodist, Pentecostal and charismatic movements, and many more. Perhaps it was happening again here?

The meetings began at seven in the evening and continued until two in the morning, six nights a week. By the weekend which marked the anniversary, numbers had reached 4,000, with over 2,000 being prayed for each night. The preaching of God's word, the altar calls and the music all impressed me, though I remained unconvinced that everything which happened came from God. I would say that some people were acting out of their own minds and emotions and imitating others rather than coming under the influence of the Holy Spirit. On the other hand I could not deny that I was witnessing a mighty and spectacular move of God which was spreading from that place out across the nations.

I was prayed for several times and once ended up on the floor, where I felt the presence of God coming in waves upon me, bringing a tremendous sense of peace. This was in marked contrast to the noisy chaos all around and I was most grateful. Later the church called for volunteers to help catch those who were falling backwards, forwards or sideways – according to how they were being 'blessed'. I found a lady who was wearing one of the official badges and offered to help. She asked for my name and when I told her, she exclaimed, 'I don't believe it! I've been looking for you for two years. Will you help me fill in my ACC forms?' Was this why I had come to Toronto, I wondered?

CBS television had arranged to interview me on the Friday evening during the meeting. First they wanted to know why a Welshman would travel halfway round the world to be at a place like that. Then the interviewer asked if I had seen anyone who had been damaged as a result of such events, either in Toronto or back home.

'I've done some research and I have to say that, to date, I haven't discovered any such damage,' I replied. 'And not a single person has come to my organisation for counselling because they have been hurt by this phenomenon.'

'Well then, can you explain what is happening?' the interviewer asked.

'Um – no!' I replied, aware of a deafening clucking noise coming from close behind me. Glancing round I saw a man from the Dutch Reformed Church shuffling round on his knees like a chicken.

The interviewer had noticed too. 'What do you think of *that*?' she asked.

I had absolutely no idea what I thought, but the grim realisation hit me that I had to say something. 'Well, perhaps we should worry when he lays an egg?' I volunteered.

The interviewer had obviously been expecting some serious biblical text, and was caught off guard by my Welsh sense of humour. Laughing, she relaxed and the rest of the interview went well, even though our conversation was accompanied by several lions, two or three eagles and a rather bizarre cockerel. When at two in the morning she decided it was time to stop recording and go home, I think we were both relieved. Never before had I been interviewed on television amid such chaos or feeling that I didn't have a single answer to give. I can only be thankful that God answered my prayer, which was that he would allow me to keep my sanity without cackling like a hyena or screeching like a parrot!

Coming home, I was looking forward to a time of calm and rest, but then I was invited to a key leaders' conference by Gerald Coates, who leads the Pioneer network of churches. They lean towards the radical, charismatic end of the spectrum – and they too had been affected by the Toronto Blessing. Within the first fifteen minutes of arriving in the meeting I could hear all the normal dogs and lions, along with crying, laughing and shouting. I noticed also a character waving a wooden stick, who went around 'blessing' individuals. Most people seemed to be on the floor in various positions – lying, crouching or kneeling. In fact I could only see three of us left standing – the other two were senior leader John Noble and Gerald Coates – obviously the three most introverted and reserved people present. John admitted rather shyly that he had not yet roared. Gerald made no comment.

I felt blessed, if confused, by the conference. We had excellent teaching and ministry, and after the emotion of the meetings, all the tired lions and chickens settled down to engage in serious, rational conversations about what God was doing and where he was taking them. By the end of the fourth and final day the man with the stick was continuing to bless people and many had received greatly from God. I could see no sign that anyone had been damaged by their unusual experiences. To sum up, I feel that there has been a major move of God and a real shaking of the church has taken place, but those who try to understand all the phenomena will have great difficulty.

When this 'blessing' first started to happen in the UK, the number of Christians asking to see us for counselling fell slightly. Some found that God had done something in them which was so deep and life-changing that they no longer needed counselling. Before long, though, we were seeing increasing numbers of those who had experienced the Toronto Blessing. They came with all the usual serious problems, but something was different. I found them much calmer. Instead of a husband and wife arriving in active conflict, they were prepared to talk about the real issues which spoiled their marriage. Those who suffered from depression told me what lay at its root and were prepared to discuss areas of sin in their lives right from the outset.

It was as though showers of rain had loosened the soil and it was much easier and less painful to pull out any poisonous roots. Problems which would have taken months of work were dealt with easily and gently, without the degree of trauma I would normally expect.

I can only conclude that the Holy Spirit has reached deep within people's minds and emotions, bringing things to the surface. Our normal emotions and cognitive thinking processes may not always cope with the deep things God wants to do in our lives. During the 'blessing' it may be that he takes our normal way of functioning off-line for a period, enabling him to touch and begin to heal very deep areas of pain. Some bizarre things may happen at this time, but afterwards order is restored again.

So has the 'blessing' done away with the need for counselling? Some churches have condemned individuals as failures for seeking counselling after being blessed. The history of God's special work in revival, though, seems to prove that counselling and pastoral care will still be needed. Earlier this century the Welsh Revival lasted only about twelve months before some churches began to close again. I believe this was partly because the needs of many were left unmet, as people were caught up in the exciting things that were happening. Just as water companies do not permanently close reservoirs because of one flood, in the same way healthy churches will keep their doors open for counselling and pastoral care even in times of great blessing. People still need opportunities to talk through their difficulties and other issues in their lives. I believe that this side of heaven we will always need to show understanding, wisdom and compassion towards those who are hurting.

Tensions in churches as a result of pastoral counselling

Over the past ten years the amount of counselling within the pastoral setting has increased considerably and I am aware that this has caused some conflicts for pastors, church leaders and others involved in church work. As with anything new there are bound to be birthing problems. I saw the same thing in Social Services when we tackled new areas in the people business, or when new departments were formed.

In my experience, the conflicts between the counselling side and management roles can be more complicated in the church setting than in any other. A number of areas can cause tension.

In order to avoid role conflicts it is vital to establish clear guidelines on the differences between counselling and ministry. Initially a person may be seen over some issues on his life's journey and in some cases these can be dealt with in the church setting by prayer and other relevant ministry. The church leadership or other appropriate person may wish to offer some care and support, but there may also be a need for ongoing counselling. In that case a contract will be made between the church member and the counsellor for say six sessions, after which it will be reviewed.

The counsellor will be accredited, under supervision and accountable to the church leadership or an appointed member, and these things should be made clear to the client so that there are no secrets. Unlike in ministry, notes can be taken and records kept on the progress of the client. Counselling would tend to be more non-directive than ministry, but if it is successful the person may come to a place where he feels whole enough to address some more spiritual and emotional issues in his life. These may well be dealt with by the pastoral care and ministry teams of the church.

There should be clear lines of communication between the counselling and ministry teams and church leaders at all times. Terms of reference should be defined within the management structure of the church so that everyone, including the client, can be clear. For example, suppose a counsellor discovers that a client is having an adulterous relationship with another church member. This is a potentially divisive matter which could affect the whole church. The counsellor must be clear whether he should inform the church leadership of such things and the client should be aware of that policy before entering into counselling.

Other dangers may come where a church is so caught up in its active vision that it tends to forget those who have deep emotional needs and who need long-term help or counselling. As a church moves on and builds and expands it must be aware that not all its members are capable of moving at the same pace. God will not be speaking to all in the same way, nor making the same demands on all. Some will not be open to God because of deep emotional hurts.

If there are two individuals with similar emotional problems it is too easy for leadership to assume that because one is healed the other will be also. Those who are not so quick to find healing may feel rejected, hurt and left out. It is advisable to have a team of counsellors and pastoral carers who can come alongside those who wish to move on but are for a time unable to, because of factors in their own lives or external environment.

Churches have some justification for feeling negative about counselling. In the early years some people found training through para-church organisations, then returned to their churches and, without consulting the leaders, started to counsel people there. In many cases they had no idea what model of counselling they were using, nor what its outcome would be. No wonder that many churches decided that anyone counselling under their authority must use the salvation model, whose only aim is to bring people to faith in Christ.

The only way for counselling to be integrated into the pastoral church setting is for it to become the responsibility of the minister, ministry team or other person appointed by the church to supervise and manage the counsellors. No matter how well accredited someone is with the ACC or BAC, it is not acceptable that they work within the church without the approval of those who have responsibility. When I worked for Social Services I had what I thought were a few good ideas about counselling children in my care, but my department told me that this was not part of my remit. As I was accountable to the managers, and counselling did not form part of their agenda, I had to accept that I would not be able to use the skills I possessed. In the same way accredited Christian counsellors have come to me over the years, complaining that they are not permitted to counsel within their church. My reply has been, 'If this is the decision of the leadership, you must respect it.'

Training and communication have improved, especially since the birth of the ACC, but we still have a long way to go. After twenty-five years of looking at counselling within the church I am more convinced than ever that training needs to be given within the local church or church organisation. In no way am I denying that para-church organisations offer good quality training, but it can isolate the trainee from his or her own church. One advantage of holding training in the local community – within a group of churches, for example – is that it helps build good relationships between the training agencies, the churches and their members. It should also ensure good standards and accountability by all. If counsellors trained in this way remain accountable at all times to the church, then counselling can work well and research shows that around 85% of cases can be dealt with in the local church setting. The rest may have to travel to specialist centres to find help.

Though at present it is unlikely that the law will require counsellors working solely within churches to be accredited, many church leaders are interested in improving standards further, and this will mean investing in people. Training and accreditation do not come cheap, in terms of either time or money. Christian counsellors often give their services without charge to their clients, but need to keep paying out for vital ongoing training and supervision. Churches need to facilitate their people in this ministry which has very real costs. It is sad that some seem to favour sending people on courses at local technical colleges, simply because they think that this absolves them of financial responsibility.

Some church groups want to set up counselling centres which reach beyond their own membership to serve the communities around them. These will require a longer training period as referrals could well come from the health authority, Social Services, education department, doctors and psychiatrists, or voluntary agencies. The counsellors will need to have more autonomy and be free to use their training models according to their clients' needs, but if the organisation is church based, they should still be accountable to a management board consisting of a mixture of people from pastoral and professional settings.

The way forward

By the year 2000 I would hope to see teams of trained counsellors working within clusters of local churches of all persuasions. However, teams from local churches will never be equipped to meet all the needs of their clients. So in addition I would like to see a network of specialist centres around the UK to which churches can send people with their blessing. The relationship between the church and this specialist agency would be similar to that between a GP and a hospital specialist, and would involve proper contracts.

I am encouraged that as these things come into place, the church will be able to find its way through the maze and fulfil its ministry of helping people more effectively.

Postscript

This book began with a bleak story of the tragic death of a fifteen-year-old boy who had become lost in the maze of his own and society's problems to which there were no simple answers. This book shows that there is a practical cost of trying to meet people's needs; the difficulties can seem overwhelming. Yet there is hope and joy too. People do come through to live and laugh again and it is wonderful to see that happen – especially for the counsellor who has played a part in helping someone find his way out of the maze and into a new place of freedom.

Julie has experienced many of the problems I have written about in this book, including a difficult marriage and subsequent divorce. Short on finance, she has struggled to bring up four teenage children on her own, and has received counselling because of serious abuse during her childhood and marriage. I know Julie well. Recently she handed me this piece which she wrote at a Christian holiday conference.

Dear Julie,
   Can you write about your thoughts? Do you love God enough to put down your feelings in writing?
   Yes, Lòrd, I will try. But how? Well, I write letters to my relatives just as I speak. Perhaps this is me speaking – me, Julie!

Julie of the plump body and hurt mind.

Julie of the 'wish I could do that' brigade.

Julie of the 'I'm too fat to live' league.

Well, I am here, Lord. What do you want from this pen?

Firstly, perhaps, I am a woman, not a piece of baggage or a man's luggage – I am *me*. I am learning to be who I am. I am learning to live with me and my body – on my own with you Lord. Yes, I have a family living with me – four young adults, each with their own problems and life to live. To them I am Mother – Mum – provider and listener, healer and encourager. So I will write this to you, Lord, not them.

Now in 1995 I am *not* being mentally or physically abused. I am recovering and learning to face life – to laugh and leap and sing with you, Lord – and one day *I will dance*.

I can appreciate the trees, the earth, the sky – one day *I will fly*!

Inside my mind are many longings, thoughts and feelings. Inside my mind are leftovers from hurts washed away. Now *I will recover*!

Lord, this year is the start of my spiritual and mental regeneration. I am learning to say 'no' and not to think I must please others. Now, Lord, I will please you and me! Hallelujah!

Lord, I will nurture spontaneity, joy, hopefulness and love. Above all, Lord, I will try to love. To love *all* human beings. What a task, Lord! To love the world, to see people as you see them, Lord, complete in their uniqueness, complete in their individuality.

This conference has opened my eyes even further to you, Lord. You've been speaking to me about spontaneity and here it is – the young, the old, the children – coming before you, Lord, with your joy and your love filling them to overflowing – the stream of your Holy Spirit overflowing through them.

Lord, teach me this lesson – to live in fullness, to dance before you, even as I sing before you, even at my age of fifty-four! Hallelujah!

Appendix
Resources

Useful organisations

Association of Christian Counsellors (ACC)
175 Wokingham Road, Reading, Berkshire RG6 1LT.
Phone 01734 662207.

Barnabas Training Consortium (BTC) and Barnabas
House, Wales
Salem Chapel, Salem Road, Johnstown, Carmarthen,
Dyfed SA31 3HJ. Phone 01267 230428.

British Association of Counselling (BAC)
1 Regent Street, Rugby, Warwickshire CV21 2PJ. Phone
01788 578328 or 550899.

CARE for the Family
136 Newport Road, Roath, Cardiff CF2 1DJ. Phone 01222
494431.

Christian Action in Research and Education (CARE)
53 Romney Street, London SW1P 3RF. Phone 0171 233
0455.

PCCA Christian Child Care
PO Box 133, Swanley, Kent BR8 7UQ. Phone 01322
667207.

Christian training centres in counselling, care and education

Barnabas Training Consortium (BTC)
Salem Chapel, Salem Road, Johnstown, Carmarthen, Dyfed SA31 3HJ. Phone 01267 230428.
A national and international training centre which offers training in counselling and care, youth work, the Children Act, legal issues, feasibility studies for potential projects, team building courses and consultancy. It is also involved in research and development.

Christian Action in Research and Education (CARE)
53 Romney Street, London SW1P 3RF. Phone 0171 233 0455.
A national caring organisation including homes programme, work within education, research into Christian issues, representation to government, basic counselling training.

Christian Counselling International
3 Charles Street, Chichester, West Sussex PO19 4EY. Phone 01243 779160.
Counselling training at advanced and basic level is offered locally. Also courses in allied subjects, including supervision.

Christians in Caring Professions (CiCP)
175 Wokingham Road, Reading, Berks RG6 1LT. Phone 01734 660515.
A professional agency offering training for those working in the professional field, particularly doctors, social workers, teachers and counsellors. Courses are held at various venues around the country.

Crusade for World Revival (CWR)
Waverley Abbey House, Waverley Lane, Farnham, Surrey
GU9 8EP. Phone 01252 783695.
Offers a range of courses on a variety of subjects, including counselling training at basic, intermediate and advanced levels. Most of their training is offered at Waverley Abbey House, which has residential facilities.

The Light House Christian Care Ministry
11 Belvedere Road, Earlsdon, Coventry, West Midlands
CV5 6PF. Phone 01203 673734.
Offers a range of courses in a variety of areas, including counselling training at basic and advanced level.

The Manna House Counselling Service
The Manna House, St Giles Street, Northampton NN1
1JW. Phone 01604 33304.
Offers basic and advanced level courses for counselling and supervision training. Some courses are arranged away from Manna House.

Network Christian Counselling
10 Cotham Park, Bristol BS6 6BU. Phone 0117 9420066.
Offers a range of courses in a variety of formats, including basic and advanced counselling training. The majority of courses are held in the Bristol area.

Philippi Trust
Philippi House, 34 Sherbourne Road, Blackpool, Lancs
FY1 2PW. Phone 01253 21859.
Offers a variety of courses, including basic and advanced level counselling training and supervision training at venues around the country.

Counselling agencies and residential care

Barnabas House, Wales
Salem Chapel, Salem Road, Johnstown, Carmarthen, Dyfed SA31 3HJ. Phone 01267 230428.
Offers residential care, day counselling, family and children work. Specialises in helping those who have been abused and those with depression, in family work and in supporting Christian leaders and professionals.

Cardiff Concern Counselling Service
Regal House, Gelligaer Lane, Cathays, Cardiff CF4 3JS. Phone 01222 664410.
Offers general counselling.

Christian Action in Research and Education (CARE)
53 Romney Street, London SW1P 3RF. Phone 0171 233 0455.
Offers a homes programme which provides residential support in private homes in times of difficulty, including some counselling support and a network of counsellors throughout the UK.

Christian Counselling International
3 Charles Street, Chichester, West Sussex PO19 4EY. Phone 01243 779160.
Offers general counselling.

The Light House Christian Care Ministry
11 Belvedere Road, Earlsdon, Coventry, West Midlands CV5 6PF. Phone 01203 673734.
Offers general counselling and specialist areas – financial, sexual problems, eating disorders.

Living Springs, The Well
105 The High Street, Stourbridge, West Midlands DY8 1EE. Phone 01384 443636.

Offers a residential unit for single mums, day counselling, pregnancy testing and pregnancy crisis counselling.

The Manna House Counselling Service
The Manna House, St Giles Street, Northampton NN1 1JW. Phone 01604 33304.
Offers general counselling.

Network Christian Counselling
10 Cotham Park, Bristol BS6 6BU. Phone 0117 9420066.
Offers general counselling.

Philippi Trust
Philippi House, 34 Sherbourne Road, Blackpool, Lancs FY1 2PW. Phone 01253 21859.
Offers general counselling and specialises in areas of addiction and abuse (sexual, multiple). Limited short-term residential facilities available.

Recommended books and other printed material

There is only space here to mention a small selection of the wide range of books available. Should any of these books prove hard to obtain, contact Barnabas Training Consortium on 01267 230428.

Roger Hurding, *Roots and Shoots* (Hodder and Stoughton).
An in-depth Christian study book on counselling models and processes. An essential reference book for the Christian counsellor. Very well written, but definitely not light bedtime reading.

Windy Dryden, *Brief Counselling* (Open University Press).
This is an excellent secular book for those starting out in

counselling. It gives very clear guidelines on the process of counselling.

John Heron, *Helping the Client* (Sage).
This secular book covers various processes and terms used in counselling. I would recommend it to those already involved in counselling and helping people.

Colin Feltham and Windy Dryden, *Developing Supervision* (Sage).
A good all round secular book for those starting out in supervision. Recommended by ACC for supervisors and counsellors.

Samuel Pfeifer, *Supporting the Weak* (World Books).
An excellent Christian book dealing with the mind and hurting people. It is written by a psychiatrist in everyday language and is suitable for pastors, leaders and counsellors.

Steve Hepden, *Rejection* (Sovereign World).
The subject of rejection is covered from childhood to adulthood. An excellent book for counsellors working in this area. It is also a useful small book to give to clients to read for themselves.

David Johnson and Jeff Van Vonderen, *Subtle Power of Spiritual Abuse* (Bethany House, USA).
An excellent book which all pastors, leaders and anyone involved in Christian counselling should read. In a clear and straightforward way it deals with the misuse of power in the church setting.

Peter Rutter, *Sex in the Forbidden Zone* (Mandela).
This secular book covers the misuse of power by professionals, doctors, therapists, church leaders and anyone in a

position of authority or power. It deals particularly, but not exclusively, with areas where women's trust has been broken during therapy, when boundaries have been crossed.

Dan Allender, *The Wounded Heart* (CWR).
A Christian book, ideal for those working with or supporting the abused. Well written, it covers all types of abuse, giving case studies and ways of helping and is therefore a very useful reference book for the counsellor. It can be used to work with a counsellee, but with caution. A work book is available.

Three Christian autobiographies dealing with working through the effects of child abuse, suitable for counsellor and client:
Cathy Ann Matthews, *Breaking Through* (Albatross Books).
Rebecca Newman, *Releasing the Scream* (Hodder and Stoughton).
Lou Lewis, *No Easy Answers* (Kingsway).

Sue Atkinson, *Climbing out of Depression* (Lion).
This easy to read, practical book is suitable for pastors, leaders and counsellors, as well as those working in the caring professions. It contains some useful guidelines for coping with depression and could be given to a counsellee or used for self help.

William Worden, *Grief Counselling and Grief Therapy* (Routledge).
A secular book – one of the best written on the subject. Helpful to those working with the bereaved and to the bereaved themselves.

Booklets

The local *Child Protection Handbook* is obtainable from Social Services departments.

The *Registration of Homes Act 1984 Policy and Procedure Handbook* is obtainable from Social Services department or Registration and Inspection Unit.

Introductory Guide for the NHS Children Act 1989 obtainable from HMSO.

Working Together (HMSO).

The Department of Health has useful booklets in layman's language which are available from BAPS, Health Publications Unit, Storage and Distribution Centre, Heywood Stores, Manchester Road, Heywood, Lancashire, OL10 2PZ. They are termed CAG 1–5 and cover:

1. *The Children Act and Local Authorities: A Guide for Parents*
2. *The Children Act and the Courts: A Guide for Parents*
3. *The Children Act and You: A Guide for Young People*
4. *The Children Act and Day Care: A Guide to the Law*
5. *Getting Help from Social Services: A Guide for Children and Young People*

In addition the following are available:

The Children Act and the Courts: A Guide for Children and Young People

The Children Act: A Guide to Help you with Day Care Registration

Counselling in the Community

Full details on setting up a counselling centre are included in *Counselling in the Community* by Roger Altman. Chapters cover counselling both in the wider community and in the pastoral church setting. There are instructions on setting up residential care, appointing supervisors, getting and providing training. Legislation covering the area of counselling is explained, and there is advice on producing feasibility studies. Sample agreements are shown, and there is a full list of useful addresses and resources.

Dr Chris Andrew, FFARCS, MRCPsych, says of the book: 'This book is very necessary, not only to encourage Christians to move strongly into this vital area of caring, but also to add some important warning notes. Roger is someone I deeply respect for the incredible amount of work he has done in raising counselling standards among Christians and for developing the quality principles of Barnabas Training Consortium. I also hold in high regard the in-depth understanding that he has of this whole field. He has covered these important issues very well. The book makes for very necessary reading and I believe should become a standard work.'

Counselling in the Community can be obtained through any Christian bookshop, direct from Kingsway Publications (freephone 0800 378446) or from the Barnabas Resource Centre, Salem Chapel, Salem Road, Carmarthen, Dyfed SA31 3HJ.